Reading, Writing & Language

Reading, Writing & Language

A Practical Guide for Primary Teachers

Second Edition

Marlene J. McCracken
and
Robert A. McCracken

Peguis Publishers
Winnipeg Manitoba Canada

Printed and bound in Canada by Hignell Printing Limited

First Edition: Thirteen Printings, 1979-1993

97 98 99 5 4 3

Canadian Cataloguing in Publication Data

McCracken, Marlene J., 1932-

Reading, writing and language

Rev. ed. – –

Includes bibliographical references.
ISBN 1-895411-70-X

1. Language arts (Primary). 2. English language –
Study and teaching (Primary). I. McCracken, Robert A.,
1926- II. Title.

LB1525.M23   1995   372.6'044   C95-920099-1

Book and Cover Design: Norman Schmidt

Peguis Publishers
100 – 318 McDermot Avenue
Winnipeg, MB
Canada R3A 0A2
toll free: 1-800-667-9673

Contents

3 How Print Works 87

4 Spelling 113

5 Independent Writing 133

Acknowledgments

"Oliver the Elephant" and "Penelope Elephant" reprinted with permission from *Move Over Mother Goose,* by Ruth I. Dowell, © 1987: Gryphon House, Inc., Box 207, Beltsville, MD 20704-0207; pages 40-41.

"At the Zoo," from *When We Were Very Young* by A.A. Milne. Illustrations by E.H. Shepard. Copyright 1924 by E.P. Dutton, renewed 1952 by A.A. Milne. Used by permission of Dutton Children's Books, a division of Penguin Books USA Inc.

"Oliphaunt," from *The Adventures of Tom Bombadil* by J.R.R. Tolkien. Copyright © 1962, 1990 by Unwin Hyman Ltd. Copyright © renewed 1990 by Christopher R. Tolkien, John F.R. Tolkien, and Priscilla M.A.R. Tolkien. Reprinted by permission of Houghton Mifflin Co. All rights reserved.

"Eletelephony" from *Tirra Lirra: Rhymes Old and New* by Laura E. Richards. Copyright 1930, 1931 by Laura E. Richards. Copyright © renewed 1960 by Hamilton Richards. By permission Little, Brown and Company.

"Rules" from *Dogs & Dragons, Trees & Dreams* by Karla Kuskin. "Rules" originally appeared in *Alexander Soames: His Poems* by Karla Kuskin. Copyright © 1962 by Karla Kuskin. Reprinted by permission of HarperCollins Publishers.

"Beside the Line of Elephants" from *Pickpocket Songs* by Edna Becker. The Caxton Printers, Ltd., Caldwell, Idaho 83605.

"Willoughby, Wallaby Woo" from *Alligator Pie* by Dennis Lee. Reprinted by permission of Sterling Lord Associates.

"The Handiest Nose" from *A Cricket in a Thicket* by Aileen Fisher. Reprinted by permission of Aileen Fisher.

"Bullfrogs" from *Ride a Purple Pelican* by Jack Prelutsky. Copyright © 1986 by Jack Prelutsky. By permission of Greenwillow Books, a division of William Morrow & Company, Inc.

"The Elephant" from *Cautionary Verses* by Hilaire Belloc. Copyright 1933 by Hilaire Belloc and renewed 1959 by Eleanor Jebb Belloc, Elizabeth Belloc, and Hilary Belloc. Reprinted by permission of Alfred A. Knopf, Inc.

"Holding Hands" from *St. Nicholas*, June 1936. Used with the kind permission of Juliet Lit Stern.

Introduction

We are pleased to revise *Reading, Writing & Language*. Since writing the first edition, we have been extremely fortunate. We have worked with thousands of teachers through workshops, and hundreds of those teachers have shared their successes, their teaching innovations, and their children's work. To this edition we have added many of their ideas and many samples of their children's work. Wherever possible we have identified the sources of the new techniques, but often we are not sure just where or when we became aware of the innovations. To all those teachers who have shared and continue to share, we say thank you. We hope they recognize that one way to continue to learn is to share ideas with other teachers.

In his introduction to the first edition to *Reading, Writing & Language*, Dr. John Downing said:

> ...this book is essentially practical...But theory and research in the psychology of learning to read would support the McCrackens every step of the way in their program. Indeed, one can go further and state confidently that the McCrackens' highly practical program is more in line with the most advanced research and theory in this field than any other book of this nature that has been written to date.

Dr. Downing died several years ago, but were he alive, we would hope that he would make the same observations about this revision. The revisions and additions are primarily practical, but we think that the research of the past fifteen years continues to support the kinds of teaching we prescribe. We are pleased that many individual teachers share their successes with us, and we are especially pleased when they report success in teaching *at risk* children. Teaching so that all children become literate is the only way to validate teaching techniques.

During the past fifteen years we have frequently used the title *Literacy through Teaching* for our workshops. We have chosen that name to emphasize the importance of *teaching* in the reading and writing programs for children.

• • •

We teach children *how* **print works** and *how* **text works.** To teach how print works, we recommend teaching children how to spell. We teach phonics as we teach spelling. This enables children to write as they learn to use phonics, putting the letters together to form words. As children write, we "nag" so that spelling, punctuation, and so on, are at their best standard. We don't demand perfection. We accept errors as part of learning. We call their spelling *temporary,* demanding that children spell as well as they can, while we teach them how to spell more correctly as they perfect their spelling.

To teach how text works, we teach children the structures of written English, teaching them how to write a sentence, how to write a paragraph, how to write a story, and so on, and we model from the best literature using the story structures and the poetic structures that authors use. Merely telling children to write sentences, paragraphs, or stories and not to worry about spelling causes frustration rather than fostering literacy.

Readers read to get messages and meanings. Before reading any text, the reader must already understand most of the ideas the text represents. So we must teach content and concepts. This way children learn enough to become interested. As we teach content we teach children how to record what they have learned and what they want to remember (note taking, for example). This writing has a child-purpose, not just a skills-learning purpose.

In the beginning stages of reading and writing, we teach much of the school day and supervise practice closely until the children have been taught enough to work independently. When children know how to spell enough and have learned a few writing structures, they can write for long periods of time without constant supervision. At that time teachers can teach a little and children can practice a lot. The teacher is free to teach small groups because the rest are writing independently.

In modernizing our schools, teaching has become the forgotten part of education. **Too often teaching is left out of the school day.** Assigning work, telling children to read and write, and then correcting mistakes does not enable children to read and write. *Children need to be taught how to read and write before we tell them to do so; they must be taught how if they are to become literate.*

Natural readers are taught at home. The teaching is so informal, such an unhurried part of home activities, that the teaching is overlooked. Natural readers are read to and with. They are sung to, chanted to, and talked with; they are taught how to explore their worlds and encouraged to do so. Curiosity is fostered. These children seem to acquire literacy with mere facilitation at school, and usually form the traditional top reading group.

With *at risk* children — children who form the bottom reading group and the remedial classes, children who have not had teaching at home — informal teaching in schools is not enough. Their natural curiosities have not been nurtured with the result that their curiosities seem dull or nonexistent. These children do not know how to learn. We must teach so that curiosity, love of learning, and literacy emerge. Hence, our workshop title, *Literacy through Learning.*

We teach children how to read, write, and spell so that they can practice; we assign practices through which children can learn what has been taught. Practice is necessary for all skill learning, but until children know how to practice and understand what they are practicing, little is accomplished.

Telling children to read and to write, while we grade, edit, admonish, or assign worksheets does little to enhance literacy.

Practicing is the natural response for a child who has learned something. Children inflict meaningful drill upon themselves. The child who learns enough to ride a tricycle just rides and rides and rides for a few days, then rides less and less, and later rides to go places or to play games. When children are learning content through their reading, they inflict practice upon themselves, recording in writing what they have learned.

We need a primary curriculum with a dual teaching emphasis:

1. content, concepts, and fact
2. language skills

The test of a curriculum is in the child's response to the question, "What did you learn in school today?" If the child says, "I learned about amphibians," while the teacher checks off in her plan book that she taught about amphibians, reviewed that *ph* sometimes spells *f,* reviewed declarative sentences, modeled paragraph writing, and assigned three writing practices for children to use, there was a good balance between skills and content. In writing, the child uses the whole of language, internalizing skills a bit at a time. The teacher teaches to review some of the partially known skills, and teaches entirely new skills in ways that enable each child to practice at a slightly more sophisticated level. **Teaching is an artful, social activity in which the teacher knows what to teach, how to teach it efficiently, how to direct practices so that every child participates, and how to get out of the way so that children can practice and learn.**

Marlene J. McCracken and Robert A. McCracken
Langley, BC, Canada
April 1995

1

Learning Language

Reading, Writing, and Language describes ways of working with language in primary grades. We believe that language has three primary characteristics:

1. Language represents meanings. This is self evident: Meanings were in early humans' brains before language evolved.

2. Language has forms. It must have form to exist. We frequently use the word *language* to mean only written text or the spoken word, but music, drama, art in all forms, TV, film, and math algorithms are all forms of language.

3. Language has three main purposes or functions: to communicate, to record meanings or ideas, and to think.

All three characteristics exist concomitantly, or there is no language. This book focuses on reading and writing, with a necessary concomitant focus on thinking, oral language, and communication. In focusing on literacy skills, a teacher's first concern must be the teaching of content. When the teacher focuses upon content, language becomes necessary and skills may be taught as needed. All literacy skills are learned and practiced meaningfully because children read to learn, and write to communicate. Traditionally, we have accepted the notion that words, not ideas, are the building blocks for reading and writing. We ask the reader to consider a different set of building blocks.

In 1979 we wrote, "If we must label *Reading, Writing, and Language* we would call it a language-experience approach to teaching English." If we must label *Reading, Writing, and Language* in 1995, we would call it "whole language." We would prefer not to label *Reading, Writing, and Language* at all, except to say it is about teaching.

CHILDREN MUST EXPERIENCE LANGUAGE TO LEARN IT

Children learn to talk without undue difficulty by listening to those around them. They learn because speech is full of meaning and is used purposefully. Children, in some marvelous ways, sort, classify, and sequence what they hear, and then begin to talk, practicing until they master speaking fairly well. As with oral language, *children must experience written language if they are to learn it* and the written language they experience must be fraught with meaning if they are to learn how to read and write. Meaning — the ideas, concepts, and content — is foremost in teaching children to use written language. Comprehension, concept building, and thinking precede a child's acquisition of skills. It is only because the text is meaningful that children can realize that they are reading and acquiring skills as they work with written language. When they understand the content, they can begin to understand how the bits and pieces, the letters, syllables, words, and sentences work. The unifying factor in language is the content.

Initially, teachers work orally with children to help them develop ideas. They present the ideas visually, in both picture and written form. Children work with the visual forms of language and gain an intuitive knowledge of the ways in which ideas may be written, and with teaching and lots of practice they begin to sense the likenesses and differences between speech and print.

CHILDREN'S EXPERIENCES PROVOKE THOUGHT

Children's experiences are the raw material for thoughts. Children need to have numerous experiences and need to be taught how to attach language to the experiences. They learn how to perceive their experiences, how to respond to their perceptions, and how to classify them. These perceptions may be classified and organized into four categories:

1. likenesses and differences
2. repeated patterns
3. growth, change, and continuity
4. interactions and interrelationships

Most disciplined study is organized this way. Spelling is organized this way. Spoken language is organized this way. One job in teaching is to make learning possible by teaching children how to perceive the information that impinges upon their brains. A second is to help teach children how to classify and organize their perceptions. Art, music, dance, drama, and so on, are natural ways for young children to explore their perceptions of the world. Teachers teach orally so that children can express their perceptions and, concurrently, they fill children with the sounds of literature. As the brain is filled with ideas through oral language and with the sounds of literature, it creates an anticipatory set for ideas and the ways in which the ideas may be expressed in print. The brain can then direct the eye to seek those ideas in text as the child learns to read.

CHILDREN MUST UNDERSTAND
THE FUNCTIONS OF LANGUAGE

In developing literacy, the teacher's job is threefold:
(1) teachers must teach children how to read and write;
(2) they must provide ways to practice so that all children
learn what has been taught;
(3) they must teach in such a way that each child comes to
understand that reading is communication with an author, and that writing is the recording or presentation of
ideas.

Children who understand that people read for information, for pleasure, to learn, and to communicate with an
author, read for these reasons as they learn to read. Eventually, children learn to recognize the words as part of this
process. If children perceive reading as pronouncing words
correctly, they may never learn to read because they pay
so much attention to the words that they cannot attend to
the meanings on the page.

COMMUNICATION SKILLS

Teaching begins with experiences, those that children
bring to the classroom, but more important, those that the
teacher provides. All children *want* to learn; the teacher's
responsibility is to see that content and concepts are
taught in such a manner that all children *are able* to learn.
As children work to learn content, they should and may
be taught skills, but the children's focus should be mainly
on the content they are learning. We often concentrate so
much upon the skills in primary grades that content sometimes seems to be forgotten. Unfortunately, skills taught
without a base in content are not learned by many children, particularly children we currently label *at risk*. By
teaching the whole class some content — for example, all
about elephants or any other animal, foods and their ori-
gins, what floats in water — the class becomes a commu-

nity of learners where all children communicate and work cooperatively as they read to learn more, and write to record what they are learning.

As the teacher teaches, providing as many ways as possible for children to learn, the children's brains are provoked to have thoughts; when children have thoughts, they innately wish to communicate, to talk to someone or to record what they are learning or perceiving. Communicating requires language, so the teacher's job is to teach the language skills needed for the children to communicate and to become increasingly sophisticated in language skills.

Communication is, simply put, the giving or getting of ideas and messages. Speech, perhaps, is the most used form of communication, and we write to record or send messages; but we also gesture, sometimes we sing or draw or dance, and if we have been taught how, we create films, videos, or we send faxes. All of these activities use language. Just a smile is language in that it has a meaning, a form, and a purpose. Similarly, art is a language; so is music. We use as many as possible forms of language as we teach a content, so that every child can get enough meaning within the brain that we can now begin to teach the child how to use the print form to read about or record those meanings. The four cornerstones of any school language program are talking, listening, writing, and reading, but we use art forms to teach young children to communicate because many ideas are easier for them to learn from art forms than from speech or print, and many young children can express their learnings easier through art than through print.

This teaching of communication skills may be represented diagrammatically as follows:

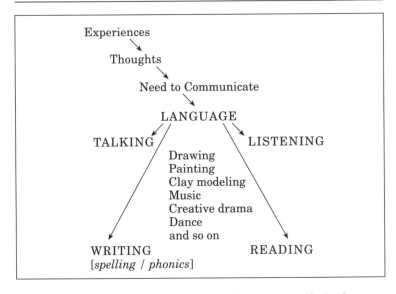

To write, a child needs to know how to spell. And so we teach children how to spell by teaching phonics. We believe some person or persons, long ago, noted the repetitiveness of the phonemes of speech and devised a way of encoding speech. By teaching phonics as a spelling skill, children can discover and understand the principle of alphabetic writing. Phonics taught through spelling can make sense to children. They come to understand that English spelling is systematic and rational even though the alphabetic system has been obscured by the use of the twenty-six-letter Roman alphabet to represent to forty-plus sounds of English. Children are able to transfer the phonics learned through spelling to reading as they need it.

PURPOSE OF READING, WRITING, AND LANGUAGE

The purpose of this book is to describe ways of teaching that will enable the teacher:

- to immerse children in oral and written language
- to have children use the language of literature as models for

practicing reading and writing
- to require children to think
- to have children understand the functions of language
- to have children acquire ever-increasing skill in using language

BASIC ACTIVITIES FOR A TEACHING DAY

There are five basic activities. These usually occur every day, providing a structure for the day:

1. Recording: Ideas are recorded mathematically, artistically, scientifically, or linguistically. As part of recording, children are taught how to spell and how to write the structures of written English.

2. Oral reading: The teacher reads orally every day for twenty minutes or more. In beginning grades this may be divided into two or more periods.

3. Sustained Silent Reading: The children and teacher read silently for a period of time.

4. Chanting and singing: These are ways of immersing children in the sounds of language.

5. Themes: Every day the teacher works seriously with an idea. It may take several days or many weeks to develop the content of one theme.

The school day is integrated by content teaching. If a teacher seriously examines a theme with children, the examination will require the skillful use of language. Children innately like to record what they are learning, and as children learn, they desire to learn more: thus, both writing and reading flow naturally from theme teaching. For years, some of the best reading and writing have been taught during science or social studies when the teacher has focused on content. Through theme teaching, teachers may teach spelling, capitalization, punctuation, and so on, as needed, while demanding that children practice those skills as they write. They may teach children how to find information and answers to questions by using a table of contents or index. Since writing and reading skills are needed, the children sense their relevance. The children come to realize the importance of skills so that they are able to accept and enjoy being taught. Relevance is not something teachers can impose; relevance is something that each child must acquire through an honest, self-felt need.

THE DIRECTION OF LANGUAGE LEARNINGS

There is a sequence in which language skills are usually taught. The sequence is repeated throughout all grades:

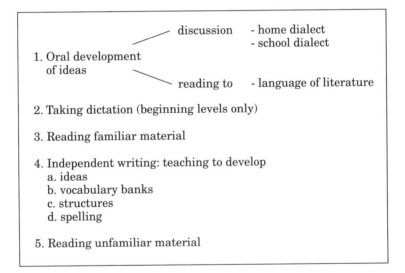

1. Oral development of ideas
   - discussion — - home dialect — - school dialect
   - reading to — - language of literature

2. Taking dictation (beginning levels only)

3. Reading familiar material

4. Independent writing: teaching to develop
   a. ideas
   b. vocabulary banks
   c. structures
   d. spelling

5. Reading unfamiliar material

All of these steps will be developed later, but some comment is needed here.

Oral Development of Ideas
Almost every lesson begins with oral work to present and develop ideas. We sometimes begin with a film, a record

or tape, or a field experience. We often begin with a book. The most important step in developing ideas is the brainstorming session where the children are encouraged to respond freely. As their teachers we must teach responsively to refine thinking and model good language. Many children will speak in a home dialect, since this is the only speech they possess, but over long periods of time, extending to grade six and beyond, they acquire other dialects.[1]

During this oral period, we record many of the children's ideas on the chalkboard, on cards, and on sentence strips. We read to the children, and provide charts of poems, songs, and prose excerpts that the children chant. From this chanting, and from the repeated hearing of longer stories, children begin to read as part of step 3, *Reading familiar material*. It is from this chanting and listening, and then reading and writing, that children begin to acquire oral command of standard English.

Taking Dictation

At the beginning of kindergarten, the teacher works orally with children to develop vocabulary, ideas, and story sense. The teacher also takes children's dictation to help them record what they have learned. The teacher reads the dictation back to the child. The purpose of this type of dictation is twofold: (1) it records the child's growth in language development and (2) it helps children realize that what they say can be written and read back. This type of

---

[1] There is concern in some parts of the United States and Canada that some children's dialects are substandard. This is an economic and political issue, rather than an educational issue. Children will learn as many dialects as they experience and practice. Most adults have several dialects; for example, a kitchen dialect, a telephone dialect, an athletic-field dialect, a good-friend's dialect, a thank-you dialect. Standard English, written and spoken, may be thought of as a dialect — a school dialect. As such, the teaching of standard English is the responsibility of the schools.

dictation continues throughout most of the kindergarten year, until the teacher believes the children are ready to make a connection between speech and print.

Late in kindergarten, or at the beginning of grade one, the teacher provokes the children to make capsule statements. Frequently, this will be a caption for a picture that the children have drawn to illustrate an idea developed during the oral period. The teacher asks children to think of one or two ideas about the topic they are learning. This way, children dictate a small amount of language, small enough that they may remember it. The teacher writes exactly what the child says, and tracks it as the child "reads" it back. After reading it back the child traces over the teacher's printing, and later moves on to copying directly underneath. *Dictation is a recording time, not a teaching time.* If the child dictates an inadequate response, perhaps saying only a single word, the teacher records exactly what the child says, recognizing that this child needs much more oral language development.

Through dictation, children learn the similarities and differences between speech and print. They learn that what they say can be written and read back. Children learn that authors write thoughts and stories, and they begin to gain insight into print as a form of language. This type of directed dictation should be relatively short-lived, covering approximately two months. Children must be taught how to write independently in grade one.

Reading the Familiar

Children who seemingly teach themselves to read at home do so by reading and rereading memorized books. This is a natural way to learn to read and in school we begin in much the same way. Children read memorized text and stories they have dictated to the teacher. Children read what the teacher has recorded on the chalkboard or on word cards, sentence strips, and charts. Children read stories that the teacher has read to them — stories for which the concepts and words have been made familiar. Children read what they have written, and they read what class-mates have written. If children have trouble with indi-vidual words when reading we say the words for them. We continue to work orally to develop concepts and vocabu-lary, and we teach spelling to develop word identification skills.

To all of this we add pocket chart work with lots of manipulation of known text so that each child can learn *how print works*. Sometimes, just reading the familiar does not seem to be enough, or by itself it takes years. Teaching with the pocket chart, having children manipu-late memorized print, quickens children's learning of *how print works*.

Independent Writing

Much of this book is devoted to independent writing. In-dependent writing does not occur automatically from dic-tation. Dictation helps children begin to understand the writing system of English, but children cannot be allowed to remain dependent on the teacher for writing. If children are permitted to dictate for too long, dictation becomes a crutch and a habit, interfering with the transition to in-dependent writing. Children need four things in order to write: ideas, words, writing structures including sentence syntax, and the ability to spell.

Children need help with ideas. They need to talk to sort out their ideas, to refine or enlarge them. They need to share ideas with others as they learn to compare and con-trast. Children probably learn more language from peer interaction than from direct adult teaching. We frequently develop vocabulary banks on the chalkboard to help chil-dren remember the ideas and the vocabulary developed during the oral work.

Grade-two class writing, following the pattern of *The Longest Journey in the World.* The text of the story is in the pocket chart, and part of their brainstorming of places for a journey is on the chalkboard.

Vocabulary banks have three primary forms:

1. A "noun" vocabulary bank

   This is a word list brainstormed and compiled for use throughout the year or with a particular theme; for example, lists of: color words; family-member words such as mother, father, uncle, aunt; holiday words for Halloween, Thanksgiving, or Christmas.

2. A manipulative language vocabulary bank

   This type of bank contains adjectives, verbs, prepositional phrases, and adverbial phrases that children need to create sentences, poetry, chants, or stories about a particular theme. It might contain a list of adjectives to describe horses, cows, or pigs as part of a farm theme, or a list of verbs describing how each of those animals might move, or a list that tells where each animal might be seen. These lists are kept on the wall for the weeks or months that the theme is being pursued.

3. A vocabulary bank for memorization
   This is the full text of poems, song lyrics, chants, and rap.
   A poem or song lyric on a chart serves as a writing
   structure as well as a word bank. A writing structure is
   anything that gives children a form on which to hang
   their ideas. Some structures are within the children
   because they have internalized a song or story through
   memorization. They have absorbed the full structure and
   the syntax of individual phrases or sentences.
   For example, *The Farmer in the Dell* serves as a
   structure on which to hang Halloween ideas:

The ghost is in the house.
The ghost is in the house.
Boo, boo! It's scaring you.
The ghost is in the house.

The same structure is available for the following:

Santa's in his sleigh.
Santa's in his sleigh.
Bringing toys to girls and boys.
Santa's in his sleigh.

Children create hundreds of songs once we teach them
how:

The cow is in the barn...
The pig is in the pen...
The snow is falling down...
The clouds are in the sky...
The tulips are popping up...
The lake is getting warm, and so on.

Spelling is discussed fully in chapter 4. Children must
be taught the basic alphabetic principle of spelling, so that
they learn how to spell. Spelling is a skill, not the memorizing of lists of words. Children need to be taught how to
sequence letters to form words, thus spelling alphabetically. When children can spell alphabetically, they will not
spell every word correctly, but they will be able to commu-

nicate in writing. If we demand perfect spelling at the onset of learning, children are incapable of writing their thoughts. They cannot use their natural language, and they will not write at much length. Demanding perfection in spelling before children have had time to be taught prevents children from learning to write and to spell. The difficult spelling patterns of the English language must be taught, but only after a child has been given a firm foundation in the alphabetic principle of English spelling.

Reading the Unfamiliar

Anyone reading this book is probably able to read fairly well in the field of education, but many teachers may not have the necessary background or vocabulary to read about surgical procedures, aerodynamics, ham radio repair, home electrical repair, and so on. The inability to read in these areas is not caused by the inability to say the words; it is in not being able to bring enough ideas to the reading.

It is common to think that a reading level is determined by the child's ability to pronounce words. However, we believe that it is primarily the ideas presented by any author that determine a book's difficulty. Therefore, the ideas expressed determine whether a child can read a book. And, the difficulty of a particular book is determined, to a degree, by the peculiar vocabulary needed to express those ideas.

Therefore, when children read in new areas, the teacher must teach to develop ideas so that the children can look at the text with sufficient apprehension to understand the ideas and the words.

READING AS APPREHENSION

Most educators, teachers, and education professors seem to accept that word recognition is a first step in learning to read. From this belief flows the pedagogy of teaching children to recognize words accurately as the first step in beginning reading. Accurate word-by-word reading, however slow, is preferred to more fluid reading with word recognition errors.

The assumption that words must be recognized before reading takes place has dominated the phonics programs, the basal programs, programmed instruction, and linguistic programs since 1950. It may have dominated programs prior to 1950, but the basal reader, as we know it today with its sequential skills programs, began in the late 1940s. Accompanying the 1950 basal readers was the insurgence of reading to dominate the primary curriculum in the 1950s. This domination continues into the 1990s.

Frank Jennings (1965) recognized the public concern when he wrote:

> What is reading? Where does it start? How can it be done well? With these questions you can make a fortune, wreck a school system or get elected to the board of education. Most people who try to think about reading at all conjure up these little black squiggles on a page and then mutter something about "meaning." If this is all it is, very few of us would ever learn anything. For reading is older than printing or writing or even language itself. It starts with the recognition of repeated events like thunder, lightning and rain. It starts with the seasons and the growth of things...Reading is the practical management of the world about us...The special kind of reading that you are doing now is the culmination of all the other kinds of reading. You are dealing with the signs of things represented. You are dealing with ideas and concepts that have no material matter or substance and yet are "real." But you cannot do this kind of reading if you have not become skilled in all the other kinds...

Despite this recognition of the importance of thoughts and concepts and "reading of the world about you," all of the published panaceas of the 1960s through the 1990s have focused upon words and how children should be taught to recognize them. Each published panacea failed to "cure-all" when practiced; 10–20 percent of children failed to become literate under even the most successful programs; other programs were disasters. With standardized test scores as the goal, several programs claimed success by citing that they had significantly better average scores. They did have the significantly better scores but they still had the 10 percent or more who failed.

This chronic failure has led us to question the assumption that children *must* recognize words accurately before they can read. We have come to view word recognition as a result of the child's having learned to read and write rather than as being a prerequisite. *Beginning reading instruction should focus on many things other than word recognition,* as suggested by Frank Jennings.

Recognizing words is merely one skill, one part of a person's use and understanding of text. Similarly, reading may be viewed as one part of a language-learning program and taught as a skill within a literacy program, a teaching program that emphasizes concepts, thoughts, thinking, and communication; a teaching program that uses dozens of communication forms and a final focus on text. Reading emerges as do the skills of spelling, penmanship, phonics, punctuation, syntax, sentence sense, recognition of story forms and poetry patterns. All emerge in an integrated way as children become literate.

Studies have shown that children who become literate with seemingly little difficulty — the children often cited as natural readers or emergent readers and writers — followed a series of recognizable overlapping steps.[2]

---

[2] See the writings of Marie Clay, Don Holdaway, Gordon Wells, and others.

1. They were born into literate homes. The adults in those homes read and wrote for adult reasons. The children saw mothers and fathers reading newspapers and magazines, saw them engrossed in novels, watched them write grocery lists, saw them typing, writing letters, using computers, and so on. Living in a literate home enabled these children to begin to realize that text is a form of language that is used for several purposes. Infants learn to distinguish speech from noise long before they begin to speak. We suspect that something similar occurs with print within the literate home, even though it is presumptuous to declare that the children recognize print as a form of language.[3]

2. Adults sang with, read with, and chanted with these infants. They took the children everywhere, conversing much of the time. The children developed many concepts about their worlds and came to understand many communication skills before they used speech efficiently or effectively.

   When any child's brain has enough meaning lodged within it, the language from the child's world gets attached to those meanings. Speech usually begins with single words; for example, a word uttered to ask for milk is used to convey a whole thought. This phenomenon also occurs with deaf infants who learn to sign if they are raised by signing parents. *Meaning within the brain precedes the acquisition of any language skill or the need for the skill.*

3. Natural readers acquired favorite bedtime stories, poems, and songs, which they demanded over and over. These were memorized and meanings were internalized. This prior understanding of the concepts and the author's exact words for expressing those concepts made it possible for the children to work with the text to discover how print works.

---

[3] This follows Don Holdaway's observation in *Foundations of Literacy* that children naturally acquire any skills that they observe adults using regularly for adult purposes.

4. At about ages two to four these children recited their favorite stories, songs, and poems to teddy bears, dogs, and any adult who would listen. They also recited to no one, just repeating stories over and over. We suspect that some children practiced silently as well as audibly so we can only guess at the number of hours they may have practiced the sounds of literature. We know that these children "read" the stories with the book open at the wrong pages and later at the proper pages; they read equally well with the book open or closed. They were not paying attention to the text as words. They were paying attention to the story, to the meanings. These children read whole books, whole poems, whole songs before they began to notice the words of the text. This fits into the notion of holistic language learning in which children go from the whole to an examination of the parts. (We are aware that this kind of reading is called *pretend reading*, but we do not feel that these children were pretending. They were reading as well as they knew how, even though they were not doing what adults do when adults read.)

5. Many children tried to write, but some ignored writing entirely as they became conscious of text. Some scribbled and asked, "What did I say?" indicating that they understood that writing (text) was a form of language. Their scribbling was an attempt to figure out how text works, just as babbling is an attempt by children to figure out how speech works. Many children imitated writing, and were taught how to write their names. At this same time they got small doses of informal, unpressured teaching about letters, letter shapes, and some bits of phonics.

6. As children became aware of the print on the page they asked questions such as, "Where does it say 'I'll huff and I'll puff and I'll blow your house in'?" Someone pointed. Or sometimes the adult tracked part of the text as he or she read orally to the child as a natural part of the reading activity. The child, with this much help, took the memorized text and worked to find out *how print works*. Usually this was a long, unhurried time without pressure to recognize the words. Somehow, children made a connection between the oral story they had heard and memorized

and the squiggles on the pages; thus began a two to three year process of figuring out *how print works.*

Proponents of phonics may say that the child used phonics, the phonics from "Sesame Street," perhaps, arguing that phonics and word recognition are the first step. We can only counter by saying that we have met young readers who knew nothing of the alphabet or phonics, and that the phenomenon described here has been noted in countries that do not use alphabetic writing. *Lengthy immersion in the sounds of text and in the world of text is the first step in creating literacy.* Word recognition is not the first step (Wells 1986; Butler 1980).

7. Through rereading memorized books and other memorized text, the children came to recognize words as a final step in reading. Comprehension was already present. It came from the repeated oral readings, and the children's participation as they were read to. The child's word recognition came from reading memorized material that was already comprehended.

We think children learn to read and continue to read through a process of apprehension as they look at text, as the brain directs the eye to seek meaning. (Apprehension has a common meaning today that implies dread, fear, or scariness. It had that meaning 400 years ago as one of several meanings. We use apprehension here in one of its oldest and still useable meanings as found in *The Oxford Universal Dictionary*, "The action of learning...grasping with the intellect...the product or the abiding result of grasping mentally..." *Webster's International Dictionary* concurs.)

We define apprehension as the mental activity that is a combination of prediction, anticipation, and expectation of the meanings, the way in which meanings are expressed, and, finally, the exact words that possibly may appear in the text.

To demonstrate this with a simple text, we ask that you read the following story. We begin with standard English spelling and format and then shift to blank spaces. Note how easily you can read most of the blank spaces. We finish the last line with a new set of alphabetic spellings. If you were a beginning reader you could check your apprehension by looking at the letters, and work at solving the mysteries of how print works.

The Farmer and the Skunk

The skunk sat under the porch.
The farmer sat on the porch.

The skunk smelled the farmer.
The farmer smelled ___ _____.

The skunk saw ___ _____.
___ farmer ___ ___ _____.

The skunk got on the porch.
___ _____ ___ __ ___ _____.

The skunk got off the porch.
The farmer got on the table.

The skunk ___ __ ___ _____.
The farmer got off the table.

The skunk ___ __ ___ _____.
The farmer got in the truck.

___ _____ ___ __ ___ _____.

___ _____ ___ ___ ___ ___ _____.

Yjr dliml hpy piy ph yjr ytivl.

You may solve the code on the last line, but the solving occurs after you have read the passage. You won't solve the words to get the message. Note how easily you read the blank spaces, as easily as if the words were in those spaces. The reading with the new set of spellings was probably much harder to read than the blank spaces.

Having to pay attention to the letters detracts from the whole process of reading. This is why we want children to memorize what they are reading before they try to solve how the letters work. (If you are a typist you can probably solve how the new spellings were devised, another form of apprehension.)

However, if you didn't know before reading that you should avoid a skunk, it is unlikely that you could read this passage even in standard English. It is unlikely that you could read this story if you didn't already know the simple story pattern of the chase. If you didn't already have in you the sound of one of the standard English sentences, article-noun-verb-prepositional phrase, you would be unable to read this. You unconsciously imposed on the text numerous expectations of the way in which the letters are used, the sequence in which words appear, and the meanings that may be expressed.

We think reading comprehension results from reader apprehension, with readers making new apprehensions when an author does not say what is expected. This process of apprehension is no more consciously done than the process of selecting words when we speak. The thoughts generate within the speaker's brain, resulting in a flow of words. Reading as an apprehensive process is neither letter-by-letter synthesis nor word-by-word recognition. The reading is idea-by-idea, glob-by-glob with word recognition as affirmation of reader apprehension.

Many children have been taught to read in a word-by-word manner with an emphasis on correct word recognition. Many of these children eventually become readers; some do not. We think that teaching word-by-word reading, whether through some phonics system or not, is inefficient, and causes some children to misunderstand what reading is. Frustrated, these children become remedial reading candidates or adults who can read but don't because it takes so long to say all the words and then figure out the meanings. Frank Smith (1982) has said that real readers read meanings directly. We would agree.

We are saying that reading must be communicative. The reader imposes an expectation on the page and receives a message. It is possible to misread, of course. But merely saying the words without receiving a message is not reading at all. *Understanding the message is reading.* We have become so conditioned to the notion that there is something called *reading* that is devoid of comprehension, that we commonly use the term *reading with comprehension.* This notion of reading devoid of comprehension implies that saying words aloud or to oneself is reading, and that once a person has learned how to read (say the words) it is time to learn to read with comprehension.

For example, you can read the following only if you already know enough to apprehend.

Using size 2 3/4 mm needles, cast on 112 sts. and work 26 rows of K.1, p.1 rib, inc. 1st. at end of last row on 2nd, 4th, 6th, and 8th. sizes only.

You have to know how to knit to be able to read this passage. No amount of phonics, or even being read to orally, will help you to comprehend what you are supposed to do. The brain has to be filled with lots of special knowledge and skill before the text can be read.

You may argue that you can read the knitting text, but that you merely cannot understand it. This is similar to Rudolph Flesch's (1955) contention when he said that he could read Czech perfectly but could not understand it at all. We disagree with this contention. Reading is understanding, or it is not reading. As teachers, we seem to assume that children understand that the words are merely a means to the end; however, many children probably infer from our teaching behavior that the words are the end. This is particularly so when the beginning reading materials have nothing in them for children to comprehend.

We are arguing that reading without comprehension is not reading. We believe the primacy of word recognition has so dominated reading instruction that most people would say, "I can read the knitting instructions. I just don't understand them." Certainly, the inability to understand the knitting directions does not mean that you need more reading instruction.

Apprehension occurs in all facets of daily life. It occurs when we listen to a lecture or to a friend speaking. Apprehension is part of seeing. I still come to a full stop two months after the installation of a traffic light that replaced a stop sign at a corner through which I have commuted daily for ten years. It matters not that the light is green. I don't see the light. I see the stop sign.

Reading as apprehension depends on several things:

- The reader has to recognize that text is a form of language; therefore it is content laden and message bearing.

- Comprehension of any language requires a storehouse within the brain of thousands of facts, concepts, and relationships before apprehension takes place efficiently.

- There must be some sort of match between what an author writes and what is already stored in the brain, or apprehension is not possible.

- The amount of practice the reader has had with text and its forms (fairy tales, short stories, cumulative stories, telephone directories, and so on) affects the reader's facility.

- The recognition of the individual words is of some importance.[4]

If teachers accept reading as a process of apprehension they should teach in accordance with that belief. If teachers no longer accept that accurate word recognition must occur before reading takes place then schools will need to change the methods and materials available.

---

[4] We are not arguing against phonics or word recognition programs. We do think some programs are more efficient than others; some are undesirable just because they take too much school time. We think that children can learn to recognize words best through a writing program in which they are taught phonics as one part of learning how to write. When learning to write and spell we pay close attention to each letter and the sounds of a word. Phonics makes sense to the writer, and its use transfers to reading as needed. Within an integrated language program there is a place for phonics, and a place for accurate word recognition. However, we view word recognition neither as the first step, nor as a prerequisite to learning to read.

2

Teaching and Learning Within the Primary Day

A primary day may be organized in many ways, but it must provide *a time for teaching* and *a time for practicing and learning.*

A TIME FOR TEACHING

How children are grouped for teaching is determined by the *purpose* of their teaching.

Teaching for thought or concept development is best done in total group because the potential interaction among twenty to thirty-five heads is greater than the interaction among five to ten heads. The more ideas there are, the more possibilities for thinking, reacting, and learning. Therefore, all activities that require sharing and expanding of thought are taught in total group situations. We realize that teaching a group of thirty primary children may be difficult. However, most children can learn to work in large groups. The learning and benefits of communication within the large group cannot be found or duplicated in small group work.

Teaching for skill development usually is best handled in small groups. Children who need instruction are grouped together for the lessons they need, and the teacher can monitor the small group closely enough to ensure successful learning.

A TIME FOR PRACTICE

Practicing is best done individually or in small groups. Children work individually to record their thoughts and to read silently. They sit in small groups for language interchange while working on projects. They do various kinds of buddy reading and writing. They work individually or in small groups in Learning Centers. Learning Centers are areas mainly for practicing skills taught by the teacher. Seventy-five percent or more of the materials in the center should have been introduced by the teacher so that children know what to do and how to do it.

THE KINDERGARTEN PROGRAM

The aim of the kindergarten program should be to develop the love of learning — to foster a curious mind. Kindergarten should be what the name means, *a garden for children*, a place where children explore language by hearing it, seeing it, and using it in many ways. It is a garden where children explore numbers, as they work with quantities and discover number relationships. In this garden they also explore the mysteries of the world they live in; they should observe, experiment, and classify their world.

The teacher's job is to teach content, to refine speech, and to fill children with the sounds of literature. Of these three, the teaching of content is the most important, because both oral language and literary language flow from, through, and around rich content. Kindergarten should develop basic concepts and understandings in many subject areas. Science, social studies, geography, math, and literature all overlap when we explore our world and encourage the intellect.

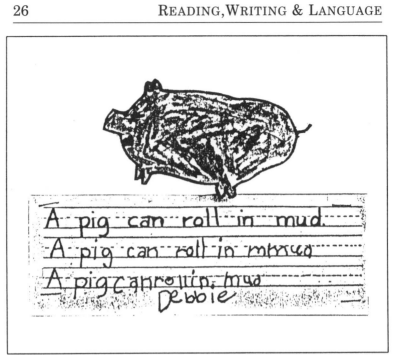

A pig can roll in mud.
A pig can roll in mud
A pig can roll in mud
Debbie

A pig can walk in the mud.
A pig can walk in the mud
A pig can walk in the mud
Jarvis

The prerequisites to success in reading and writing are being able to think, being able to sense the patterns of the language, and being able to express oneself orally with reasonable clarity. Kindergarten should be an oral program of exploration that develops thinking, sensitivity to written language, and oral communication.

BEGINNING GRADE ONE

Beginning grade one is perhaps the most exciting time in a child's life. Most children come to grade one believing that they will learn to read and write, and are eager to begin. Some are worried because they have already known failure personally or they have learned about school failures from older children.

The challenge to first-grade teachers is formidable. We must meet the children's expectations, by teaching them to read and write. If disappointed, the children will lose their interest and excitement and they will fail to learn. We must teach so that learning is natural for every child. The procedures and requirements must show all children that they *can* learn and that learning is joyful. Verbally assuring children that they can learn is not enough; nor is extrinsic reward. We must teach in such a way that all children realize that they *are* learning. *The key to successful teaching and learning is this: Teach in ways that enable each child to successfully practice what has been taught so that they all learn.* Follow-up each lesson with learning activities that suit both the interests and abilities of the children. This teaching provides a program that offers both challenge and security.

Good teaching challenges each child to think, to discuss, and to share thoughts. *Good teaching provides security* so

Left: The kindergarten class studied pigs as part of a Farm Theme. The children each drew a pig, dictated to teacher about what a pig can do, and copied under teacher's printing as part of learning to write. Ed. note: These were very colorful pigs — bright pink and yellow!

that all children sense that their thoughts are worthwhile, so worthwhile that they are used by the teacher and other children. *The teacher provides security* by assigning practices suitable for differing abilities so that every child may practice and learn without frustration.

> *Good teaching challenges* each child to work with text and *provides security* by having children begin by reading their own thoughts written down, or by using memorized text.
>
> *Good teaching emphasizes* that language learning is a social, non-competitive activity. Sharing, with groups helping one another, creates security and freedom.

The first few weeks of grade one are most successfully handled trough total group activities and instruction. The teacher gets to know the children, but, more important, the children get to know the teacher, the room, the school environment, and the teacher's expectations. Children also learn how to do activities before they are required to work independently in small groups or by themselves. The beginning weeks are the time when the children are taught what the teacher expects, how to use materials, how to record, how to discuss, and how to behave. *This is the time when children learn that they are free to learn in any way that suits them, but that they are not free not to learn, nor to deter others from learning.*

This is the time when expectations and procedures are clearly demonstrated so that all children will have the security of knowing what to do and how to do it when they begin to work without direct teacher guidance. *Children must know what to do and how to do activities before they can work independently.* Until children know how to work independently it is futile for teachers to attempt individual or small group instruction because they will be interrupted incessantly with questions from frustrated children who want to learn and can't. The physical activity of young children is directly proportionate to mental activity. The child who is engrossed in thinking and learning is relatively inert. The child who wants something to think about or something to learn about is moving around exploring and talking. Discipline problems are created when we do not teach children *how* to work before requiring them to work, or when we give children work that is inappropriate to their abilities.

THE PRIMARY GRADES

This book stresses the importance of thinking, and the two aspects of communication — the giving of thoughts and the getting of thoughts. There are three major types of activities:

1. activities to promote thought, to develop needs and desires to communicate, and the desire to record one's own thoughts

2. activities that teach the ways to record thoughts and the ways to practice thinking or learning

3. activities that teach children how print works and allow children to begin the natural process of learning to read and write

Through good teaching, children come to several understandings. Teaching so that children reach these understandings is the goal and purpose of education. They are not intended to be formally memorized and recited.

Goals

Good teaching strives to teach children
• that their thoughts are important
• that they can learn from the thoughts of others, particularly from their classmates and from authors
• that their thoughts can be recorded in many ways
• that writing is much like talk printed down
• how to do their own writing even though their beginning attempts are imperfect

- how to read their own recorded thoughts and the recorded thoughts of others
- by filling them with good literature so that the osmosis of language and ideas occurs
- so that they can absorb, almost intuitively, the structures of written English
- to reflect on the ideas of authors and to apply those thoughts to their own lives
- to have empathy with characters
- to think
- to understand *how print works*

Children taught this way take pride in their work, take pride in themselves, and take joy in communicating from their own writing and reading. They develop an independence of thinking that reflects enough conformity to communicate and sufficient independence to be interesting, and they develop an understanding of how language functions.

One second-grade, seven-year-old boy who had been taught this way for two years was directed, during an individual reading test, to "read a word list." He replied in an inflected voice conveying incredulity, "Who would ever read a word list?" When asked to pronounce the words on the list he did so, but added before beginning, "Why would anyone *ever read* a word list?" A five-year-old boy finishing kindergarten was asked, "Can you read?" He replied, "I can read books, but I can't read any words yet." Both boys demonstrated that they had learned important concepts — concepts that they had learned intuitively through a teaching program in which the goals, the teaching, and the learning activities were consistent and not hypocritical.

NATURAL LEARNING — EMERGENT READERS

The 1980s saw a resurgence of interest in natural learning. This was evidenced by (1) the whole language movement, (2) a greater emphasis upon thematic teaching of reading and writing, (3) the *process writing* movement, (4) the shift within basal readers to literature, and (5) the resurgence of *ungraded primary* units. None of these is new, but some of the labels applied to them are, and there seems to be greater public and educational establishment acceptance of a variety of programs. There is no single accepted definition for these programs; rather they seem to be based on varying notions of how children acquire language and on a disenchantment with the skills approach of the basal readers from the 1960s through the 1980s. Within this change is a common desire to allow the child to learn naturally and holistically, as opposed to making the child fit methods and materials. However, there does not seem to be consensus as to how this is to be done.

Most teachers and many adults have known a child or several children who seem to have taught themselves to read. They come to school already reading and writing, and they learn easily regardless of the methods used in kindergarten and grade one. We call these children *Esmeralda*. Most teachers have also known many children who come to school with no knowledge of reading and writing, not speaking much, and knowing nothing about print or books. We call these children *Matthew, Mark, Luke,* and *John*; they are sent to school to teach teachers how to teach. The test of any school program is not how well the Esmeraldas learn, but what happens to the Matthews. The current label for Matthews is *at risk*.

We have come to accept the research findings of Gordon Wells (1986). He found that all children learn language and language skills by going through the same stages. He reported that I.Q., home background, letter knowledge, and so on — the attributes traditionally cited as important for reading success — were not important. He cited a single factor, how many times the child had been read to, as critical in a child becoming literate. The New Zealand research, led by Marie Clay (1972; 1979), corroborates Wells' finding that all children go through similar stages. These are consistent with our own experiences with children.

In 1966 Dolores Durkin reported about children who came to school reading. She reported one common factor among all the children studied; someone had read to them. Durkin did not single out this factor as singularly important, nor did she attempt to quantify the amount of *reading-to* the children had. Dorothy Butler, in *Cushla and Her Books* (1980), affirms the importance of being read to. Both Wells and Butler indicate that children need to be read to thousands of times if they are to come to reading naturally. M.J. Adams (1990) affirms this also, saying that children who have been read to in excess of 1000 hours come to print easily.

We have observed Esmeraldas coming to print at ages three, four, and five. Their biographies have striking similarities. They went home from the hospital and were talked with, sung to, chanted to by mother and father, and numerous other members of their families. They were carried everywhere and were smiling, gurgling participants in the verbal world of adults. They learned to speak because they were talked to and with. Esmeraldas' mothers and fathers sang or chanted every time a diaper was changed. Esmeraldas were read to and sung to as part of bedtime routine, and by the age of three or four had listened to stories and poems hundreds of times. They demanded a favorite bedtime story fifty or more times. Wrath descended upon any adult who misread a word during the bedtime ritual. Esmeraldas took that favorite bedtime story and read it to their dog, their stuffed animal, to anyone who would listen. They "read" equally well with the book open or closed. They paid little or no attention to the text; they read the whole book from memory.

And then the miracle of discovering how print works began. Esmeralda took her favorite book and, knowing what it said, was able to work with the text and figure out the words. She didn't figure them out instantly or all at once, but over a period of a year or two she returned to her favorite books and looked at that memorized text, discovering the connection. She had marvelous, loving, informal teaching for three or four years. Mother or father occasionally pointed to the text, and people occasionally answered her questions about the text. Parents like to believe that Esmeralda was self taught, but she had the best of one-on-one teaching, without pressure to perform or to prove that she was learning. She had hundreds of informal teaching sessions, and she worked hundreds of times to solve the mysteries of print.

The Matthews of our world have had none of this teaching. They come to school ignorant of print, the world of literature, and the marvels of the world about them. It is no wonder that they fail when we assume that all they have to do is *follow along* the print and learn the alphabet and the sounds. The alphabet is meaningless to them, as is all text. They cannot follow along any more than Esmeralda followed along when she began to look at books at one or two years of age. She could not follow along until she had listened for three or four years as the sounds of stories and poetry filled her brain.

We are not saying that Esmeralda learned by a look-say method, or that she did not use phonics. We are saying that she used a multiplicity of ways, all of which we do not pretend to know at this time. We also know that *she developed understandings about text and stories before she was concerned with the bits and piece*s, the letters, or words.

Gordon Wells (1986, 156–157), explains the importance of understanding how written language works as readiness for literacy:

> In most writing...there is no context in the external world to determine the interpretation of the text. The aim must therefore be to use *words* to create a world of meaning, which then provides the context in terms of which the text itself can be fully understood. To understand a story

therefore — or any other written text — the child has to learn to give full attention to the linguistic message in order to build up a structure of meaning. For, insofar as the writer is able to provide cues for the reader's act or construction, he or she does so by means of the words and structures of the text alone.

What is so important about listening to stories, then, is that, through this experience, the child is beginning to discover the symbolic potential of language: its power to create possible or imaginary worlds through words — by representing experience in symbols that are independent of the objects, events, and relationships symbolized and that can be interpreted in contexts other than those in which the experience originally occurred, if indeed it occurred at all.

Compared with the longer-term effects of this discovery, it is easy to see why drawing, or matching names or sounds to the letters of the alphabet, although useful, is of much less significance for later progress at school. The same is true of learning that takes place when looking at picture books or catalogues and discussing the names and attributes of the objects depicted. No doubt this activity helps children to enlarge their vocabularies — at least for those things that can be pictured. It also gives them practice in answering display questions of a limited kind, and this may well give them an initial advantage if they find themselves — as many do — in classrooms where such skills are emphasized...

This interpretation of the connection between early experience of listening to stories and later educational achievement is confirmed by the final part of the investigation...

The results were clear-cut. Only the frequency of listening to stories significantly predicted the teachers' assessment of oral language ability...

We have come to believe that natural learning is philosophically different from look-say or phonics or any of the basal-reader programs of the 1950–1990 time period. In all those programs there is a consensus that to read, children must recognize words and that they must be taught to recognize all the words as they read. M. J. Adams (1990), in her summary of research about beginning reading, reflects this belief. This is hardly surprising since more than 95 percent of the summarized research presumes that words must be taught before reading takes place. Her conclusions therefore support the teaching of word recognition as the core need in beginning literacy, and imply that this can be best done through phonics. Most grade one and two standardized tests are tests of word-recognition, even those labeled as tests of reading comprehension. It should not require research to prove that children who are taught a systematic way of pronouncing words do better on tests of pronouncing words than those children who are not taught in this manner. If we believe that the central need for developing literacy is something other than pronouncing words correctly, then the conclusions of Adams' summary are not necessarily valid.

We are saying that Esmeralda used a different philosophy, albeit intuitively. For her, the most important factor in reading stories and poems was that she enjoyed them — they made sense and sounded the way stories should sound. She didn't use phonics to read the fairy tale beginning "Once upon a time." But she did use a little bit of phonics to know that "Long ago and far away" was not "Once upon a time." We suspect that Esmeralda learned how print works from reading and rereading known stories imperfectly until word recognition was as automatic as it is with adults. We do not accept the notion that automatic word recognition is learning words through some phonics method that results in the smooth blending of letter sounds, done so fast within the brain that we are unaware of it.

The alphabet and phonics are tools. However, they are necessary and more useful for the writer than for the reader, and phonics can be more effectively taught and learned through a spelling and writing program than through a reading program. Letters and letter sounds make sense as part of a spelling program as children learn to encode the sounds of each word they want to write. Since the phonics learned through spelling makes sense, children transfer the use of phonics to reading as needed. We prefer to delay the formal teaching of writing and spelling until grade one, and feel that it must be delayed for the Matthews until they have been filled with at least a kindergarten year of language.

THREE STAGES OF NATURAL LEARNING

We think that children grow into literacy in three natural stages. We have labeled these stages (1) *pre-reading*, (2) *beginning reading*, and (3) *reading*. Although pre-reading includes all the years before kindergarten as well as what we do in school, it is the kindergarten year where children are filled with language. Many Matthews would benefit from two years of language filling. Beginning reading is the nitty-gritty stage where children learn how print works, and reading is forever as children become more practiced and more sophisticated. The three stages overlap, of course.

Pre-Reading

In pre-reading children learn how stories and poetry sound, and they learn many of the forms of literary English. The learning is intuitive, and the teaching almost totally informal. With Esmeraldas the teaching was almost always informal. It occurred naturally in a literate household as part of the daily routine of child-raising. We now hear about emergent literacy as a new discovery. The name is new; the phenomenon is not. The emergence was caused by teaching. *It still must be caused; it is not just the result of a child being given enough time.* Children must be taught for two reasons:

1. Neither society nor schools will tolerate children taking four to five years to emerge after they enter school. We think of Esmeraldas as brilliant, seemingly forgetting the amount of teaching and the amount of time they took to become literate. Matthews are no smarter than Esmeraldas. They will not emerge faster unless we teach directly and efficiently in ways that enable them to learn faster.

2. The Matthews themselves will not tolerate being illiterate for their first four years of school. They know that other children are learning and that they are not. *Matthew is normal but he is untaught*: no normal child can tolerate years of failure. We must teach so well that we provide for Matthew what Esmeralda's family provided leisurely and informally.

First, we must read to Matthew, and we must provide every possible opportunity for Matthew to engage in languaging activities. Matthew must be read to at least twice a day in school, preferably more. We can do this only if we, as teachers, take time to select the best children's literature and give precious school time to the act of reading to children. We must find many additional ways to fill these children with literature. We can do this in several ways:

[handwritten margin notes: 1. Read to at least twice a day • best of literature]

• Get reading buddies from upper grades who come and read with children one-to-one. This can be a regular part of each school day, or before or after school. These reading buddies are often the Matthews of grades five and six.

• Get the best of children's literature on audio and video tape that children can listen to. Weston Woods Studios[1] has fine materials available for this kind of reading.

---

[1] In the United States write: Weston Woods Studios, Weston, CT 06883. In Canada write: 60 Briarwood Avenue, Port Credit, ON L5G 3N6.

- Teach parents the importance of reading to their children every day. There are many programs that have successfully trained parents how to read bedtime stories to their children.

- Teach in ways that allow children to work with text as Esmeralda did, reading books from memory. *Reading, Writing, and Language* describes these ways.

- Provide the best children's books for them to use in a comfortable, social setting. We should provide extensive classroom libraries so that books are part of the immediate environment, and we routinely allow children to borrow books for overnight reading. What we do and what we have in the room tells our children what we prize. We know teachers who have more than 500 trade books in their classroom libraries even though there is a large library down the hall.

Much of a child's learning is holistic and much of a child's initial learning is through the emotions. We think that emotionally secure people are better able to learn than emotionally insecure people. Children, particularly, need emotional security if they are to learn easily or optimally. Sylvia Ashton-Warner (1959; 1963) recognized this in her concern for organic learning. Rachel Carson (1956, 45) recognized this in her writing about her nephew Roger:

> I sincerely believe that for the child, and for the parent seeking to guide him, it is not half so important to know as to feel. If facts are the seeds that later produce knowledge and wisdom, then the emotions and the impressions of the senses are the fertile soil in which the seeds must grow. The years of early childhood are the time to prepare the soil. Once the emotions have been aroused — a sense of the beautiful, the excitement of the new and the unknown, a feeling of sympathy, pity, admiration or love — then we wish for knowledge about the object of our emotional response. Once found, it has lasting meaning. It is more important to pave the way for the child to want to know

than to put him on a diet of facts he is not ready to assimilate.

Bruno Bettelheim (1976, 18–19) discussed the value of old fairy tales in emotional development:

> For a story truly to hold the child's attention, it must entertain him and arouse his curiosity. But to enrich his life, it must stimulate his imagination; help him to develop his intellect and to clarify his emotions; be attuned to his anxieties and aspirations; give full recognition to his difficulties, while at the same time suggesting solutions to the problems which perturb him. In short, it must at one and the same time relate to all aspects of his personality — and this without ever belittling but, on the contrary, giving full credence to the seriousness of the child's predicaments, while simultaneously promoting confidence in himself and his future...
>
> This is exactly the message that fairy tales get across to the child in manifold form: that a struggle against severe difficulty in life is unavoidable, is an intrinsic part of human existence — but that if one does not shy away, but steadfastly meets unexpected and often unjust hardships, one masters all obstacles and at the end emerges victorious...
>
> Explaining to a child why a fairy tale is so captivating to him destroys, moreover, the story's enchantment, which depends to a considerable degree on the child's not quite knowing why he is delighted by it. And with the forfeiture of this power to enchant goes also a loss of the story's potential for helping the child struggle on his own, and master all by himself the problem which has made the story meaningful to him in the first place. Adult interpretations, as correct as they may be, rob the child of the opportunity to feel that he, on his own through repeated hearing and ruminating about the story, has coped successfully with a difficult situation. We grow, we find meaning in life, and security in ourselves by having understood and solved personal problems on our own, not by having them explained to us by others.

Children, in asking for an old tale over and over again at bedtime, are learning. It is not obvious what they are learning, but we do not think it is the facts of the story. They know the facts. Their need is emotional: their learnings are through empathy, and their learnings are discovering the sense of mystery, awe, or wonder, to use Rachel Carson's phrase. Children in school need this same kind of repetition where they may safely identify with the characters in a tale, empathize with the character's dilemma, and explore whatever mysteries challenge them.

Teachers need not worry if children are comprehending when they are attending. The human brain cannot pay attention when it is not learning, nor can it fail to attend when it is learning. Five-year-old children are learning when they are paying attention. We need to make judicious choices in what we teach, and then have faith: if the children are attending, they are learning important things even though we cannot test their learnings. When children are inattentive the task is either too hard or too easy, and we need to adjust the content and/or the teaching.

Memorizing Books

Some of the books we read to children should be books that are easily memorized so that Matthew can begin to do exactly what Esmeralda did. In kindergarten, Matthew must memorize ten books, ten or more poems, and twenty or more songs, so that the sounds and sense of literature are in him. Without this memorization, it is unlikely that we can teach him *how print works* as part of *beginning reading*.

Oral work, through which children explore the ideas of stories, songs, and poetry, is the heart of the kindergarten language program. From this program children learn about books and stories; they learn about story structures and develop apprehension for text. They use this apprehension later as they work with the stories and poems they have memorized to develop word recognition. Their most important learning is that books are a source of knowledge and pleasure.

We suggest there are six types of books that children find easy to memorize. Although one book may fit into more than one category, knowing each type helps provide a healthy literary diet. All titles mentioned are listed in the Bibliography of Books for Children, page 285.

Rhythmic Books

Most children's poetry is rhythmic as is much of children's prose. The power of rhythm cannot be overstated. By its demanding nature, it forces children into learning exact words. Even when hearing a poem for the first time children anticipate some words and know automatically what is coming because only one word or phrase will fit into a particular context.

Leland B. Jacobs' book, *Good Night, Mr. Beetle,* is a classic example of this type of book. Cover the text below, and then expose one line at a time to discover how you can read one or two of the lines before you see them.

Good night, Mr. Beetle,
Good night, Mr. Fly,
Good night, Mrs. Ladybug,
The moon's in the sky.

Good night, Mr. Robin,
Good night, Mrs. Wren,
Good night, Mrs. Sparrow,
It's bedtime, again.

Good night, Mr. Rooster,
Good night, Mrs. Sheep,
Good night, Mr. Horse,
We must all go to sleep.

Good night, Miss Kitten,
Good night, Mr. Pup,
I'll see you in the morning
When the sun comes up.

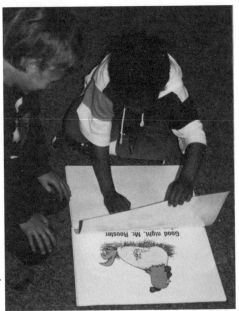

Children engrossed in re-reading *Good Night, Mr. Beetle* from a big book.

Jack Prelutsky has written two books of children's nursery rhymes, *Ride a Purple Pelican* and *Beneath the Blue Umbrella*. Both are filled with delightfully rhythmic poetry that, once heard, creates almost instant memorization. For example:

> Bullfrogs, bullfrogs on parade,
> dressed in gold and green brocade,
> scarlet buttons on their suits,
> fringes on their bumbershoots.
>
> See them tip their satin hats
> as they bounce like acrobats,
> hear them croak a serenade,
> bullfrogs, bullfrogs on parade.

Children who have learned several of Prelutsky's poems have a head start when letter-sounds are taught. For example, the letter *b,* the sound /b/, is part of *bullfrogs, bumbershoots, acrobats, buttons* and *brocade.* /b/ now has the possibility of making sense.

Most children know Karla Kuskin's *Bugs* after a single hearing.

I am very fond of bugs.
I kiss them,
And I give them hugs.

We have written *Children's Alphabet*, which can be chanted or sung. Four pages are produced on the following page.

Most teachers are required to teach the alphabet and the letter sounds as part of the kindergarten program. Using the *Children's Alphabet* teaches the alphabet through chanting or singing. Children further explore the letter sounds by substituting their own names and additional toys to create their own alphabet books.

Repetitive Books

Every literate adult can remember some favorite childhood stories, and, most likely, several of them will have repetitive parts that can still be recalled with little effort.

I recall without effort, yet with no memory of when I learned:

Run, run, run as fast as you can.
You can't catch me. I'm the gingerbread man.

Piggy won't go over the stile
And I shan't get home tonight.

I'll huff and I'll puff and I'll blow your house in.

Halfway up the stairs is the stair where I sit...

(Several others will no doubt pop into your mind from memories of childhood.)

Lots of children's favorite books have repetitive parts that children learn almost instantly. They join in the repeated part each time it occurs in the story. They chime in with the wolf in *The Three Little Pigs* each time he says, "I'll huff and I'll puff, and I'll blow your house in."

Allison has an astronaut,
an astronaut, an astronaut.

Allison has an astronaut
to play with all day long.

Byron has a baseball bat,
a baseball bat, a baseball
bat.

Byron has a baseball bat
to play with all day long.

Yolanda has a yo-yo,
a yo-yo, a yo-yo.

Yolanda has a yo-yo
to play with all day long.

Zelda has a zebra,
a zebra, a zebra.

Zelda has a zebra
to play with all day long.

Children may join and sing the following as many as twenty-six times in a single reading of George Shannon's modern classic tale, *Lizard's Song:*

Zoli, zoli, zoli
Zoli, zoli, zoli.
Rock is my home.
Rock is my home.

Children repeat in the same way in the old folk tale of the gingerbread boy:

Run, run, run
as fast as you can.
You can't catch me.
I'm the gingerbread man.

We recommend all the old tales that have easily memorized, repeated parts. When children begin to investigate text at the beginning reading stage, they somehow recognize the repeated text. Repeated print is often the first bits of print that children analyze as word recognition begins. We are not prepared to explain this phenomenon; it is what Esmeraldas do. It is what we must teach Matthews to do.

Further, well-written tales challenge children by their vocabulary and sentence structures. Simplified texts make reading difficult, if not impossible, for two reasons. The syntax is forced rather than natural, and the simple text often removes the inherent emotional appeal that makes the story meaningful to the child.

We commend the following more recent books as excellent for their repetition and for their emotional appeal to children:

Hattie and the Fox by Mem Fox
Good Night, Owl by Pat Hutchins
Once: A Lullaby by bp nicol

Lizard's Song and *Dance Away* by George Shannon
The Cow and the Elephant by Claude Clayton Smith
Spider on the Floor, Little Fish, and *Little Yellow Duck* by
　　Robert A. and Marlene J. McCracken

Cumulative Books

The House That Jack Built, a Mother Goose tale, is perhaps the first recorded cumulative story in English. It has been the model for many stories since then. Cumulative books allow long stories to be memorized so that children can work with a large amount of text. (The authors of basal readers have frequently limited the number of words in the stories written for beginning reading instruction. But limiting the number of words does not necessarily make learning to read easier.) We think that children may see text as a puzzle; we teach so that children can work meaningfully with the puzzle. Sometimes puzzles with lots of pieces are easier than puzzles with just a few pieces.

The following are several recent cumulative books that children love and find easy to recite from memory or from looking at the pictures.

Shoes from Grampa by Mem Fox
Fat Cat by Jack Kent
The Big Red Barn, The Big Red Apple, Fat Pig and *The
　　Old Woman and the Pig* by Robert A. and Marlene J.
　　McCracken
　The Jacket I Wore in the Snow by Shirley Neitzel
　The Old Woman Who Swallowed a Fly, traditional
　My Cat Likes to Hide in Boxes by Eve Sutton
　The Napping House by Don and Audrey Wood
　The Judge: An Untrue Tale by Harve Zemach

Basic Sentence Pattern Books

Basic sentence pattern books are usually not literary, and they can be mundane and boring. Most are ones that children can read from the pictures alone, and Esmeraldas loved them at ages three and four.

Basic sentence pattern books have a limited use in developing literacy. They should be no more than 10–15 percent of a teaching program, even with children learning English as a second language. These books get things started, but children with limited English remain limited if we use a majority of basic sentence pattern books that use simple patterns of speech, rather than the rich patterns of literature and books.

Dick Bruna has created several simple books for young children. His books have an exquisite sense of children's natural language, their love of economical pictures, and humor for three- to five-year-olds. His book, *My Shirt Is White*, is a perfect book for children, as is *The Dog*.

Lois Lenski's *Mr. Small* books have charmed children for years with their simple language patterns and economical illustrations. Many adults wonder what children see in these simple books, but children enjoy them tremendously. They find the books suited to their needs.

We have written several books that use basic sentence patterns in repeatable ways. We have tried to teach something as well as merely repeat the basic sentence patterns. One of our simplest is *I Am a Pirate*. The first few pages are shown on the following page. *I Am a Kindergartner*

In the fall, kindergarten children in San Bernardino, California memorized *I Am a Pirate*. They read the book and chanted it several times from memory. They used the pattern to chant about themselves in their school clothing — My shoes are brown. My socks are green...(and so on) — and made illustrated books.

In November, each drew what they wanted to be for the following Halloween, using the pattern of *I Am a Pirate*. Each child drew a favorite costume. The teacher put the children's pictures through the copier so that children could make books about their costumes by coloring their pictures. Our favorite was *I Am a Butterfly*, reproduced on page 49 without the original color. Philip's book, shown on page 50, is more representative of kindergarten children.

I AM A PIRATE

My eye patch
is black.

My hat
is orange.

My bandana
is red.

My belt
is yellow.

My boots
are brown.

Children enjoy simple, basic speech pattern books as one way of learning about words and as books in which to practice reading and recognizing words. Children can instantly learn how to chant *One Pig, Two Pigs*, two pages shown below, and then use the pictures to remember the text as they learn the words.

We find these books most useful as writing patterns, however, where children expand beyond the books. In initial writing, children can use the structures to write individual books or individual pages for class books. This gets writing started both quickly and successfully. For example, children can write using the pattern of *What Is This?* (See representative pages on page 53.) They need to read the book together with the teacher, learn how to write three words, *This is a*, and to draw a picture.

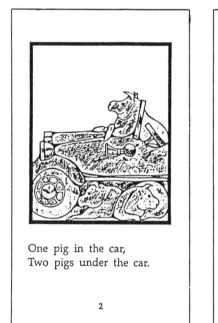

One pig in the car,
Two pigs under the car.

2

One pig in the box,
Two pigs under the box.

3

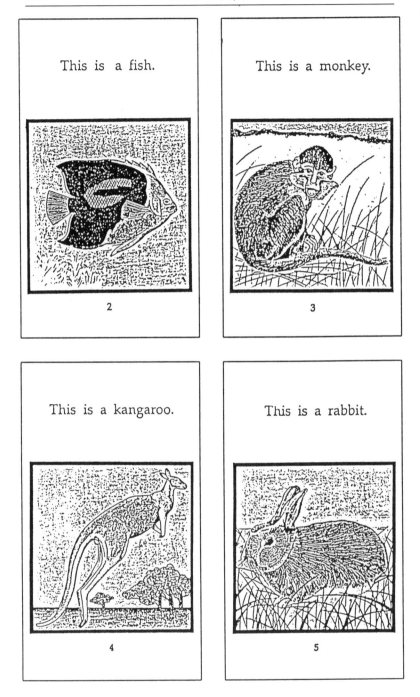

This is a fish.

This is a monkey.

2

3

This is a kangaroo.

This is a rabbit.

4

5

Two-Part Books

There are not as many two-part books as there are other types, but they are one of children's favorites. Children read these stories as drama or conversations, making themselves part of the book. Reading, even chanting with the class, may seem to be a solo to some children. Two-part books are conversations.

The classic book of this type is Robert Kraus's *Whose Mouse Are You?* It begins:

Whose mouse are you?
Nobody's mouse.
Where is your mother?
Inside the cat...

Brown Bear, Brown Bear, What Do You See? by Bill Martin Jr., is a kindergarten classic. Mirra Ginsburg's *Where Does the Sun Go at Night?* is an old Russian tale that children love. It answers their eternal questions in a child-like way that is emotionally perfect. Ginsburg's *The Chick and the Duckling* with its repeated "'Me, too,' said the chick" is perfect in meeting children's need to do everything.

We have several question-and-answer books that children enjoy. Two of them, *Where Do You Live?* teaches about animal habitat, and *What Do You Have?* teaches about animal attributes (pages shown on pages 54–55). Both are simple writing patterns that children use to gain control of writing structures.

Children use this pattern to record new knowledge. An Oakland, California grade 1-2 class recorded what they were learning about dinosaurs as shown on page 56.

Do you have
a large beak?

1

No! No! No!
Birds have large beaks.

2

Do you have a long,
grey trunk?

11

No! No! No!
Elephants have long,
grey trunks.

12

Do you hare a long hard tale and spikes?

No! No! No! a ankylosaurus has a long hard tale and spikes

Do you have large bony plates down your back and a brain like a walnut?

NO! NO! NO! Stegosaurus has large bony plates down his back and a brain like a walnut.

DO you have a Beak Like a Parrot and a Bony Coller?

NO! NO! NO! Protocera-ratops hase a Beak Like a Parrot, and a Bony Coller.

   Some Dogs Don't (two pages shown below) is a simple two-part book that allows children to read their part on a first reading. It was used in Bonnie Addison's grade-three class to initiate writing with a group of children who thought they couldn't write. The example on page 58 shows how a simple frame or structure can give children the ability to say much more than they could without the crutch.

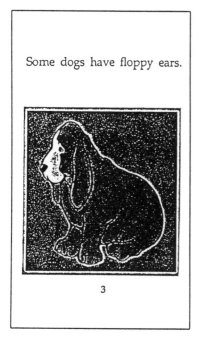

Some dogs have floppy ears.

3

Some dogs don't.

4

Some kids have single
     parents
Some kids don't.

Some kids have lds offriends.
Some kids don't.

Some kids read books,
Some kids don't.

Some kids have dogs,
Some kids dont.

Some kids win,
Some kids don't.

Some kids phy hockey cards
Some kids don't.

Some kids love there sisters
Some kids don't.

Some kids can count,
Some kids don't.

Some kids ride bikes.
Some kids don't.

Some kids have foster moms
Some kids don't.

Some kids know how to write.
Some kids don't.

Some kids have sisters.
Some kids don't.

Some kids speack inglish.
Some kids don't

Some kids colour neatly
Some kids don't.

Some kids have healthy legs
and arms.
Some kids don't.

Some kids have lite skin.
Some kids don't.

By kenneth

The Fly in the Barnyard, shown below and on the next page, is a question-and-answer book that teaches children the names of the parts of various animals. It enabled grade-one children in Mrs. Forsell's class in Aurora, Illinois to do partner writing, creating the kind of response shown on pages 61–63.

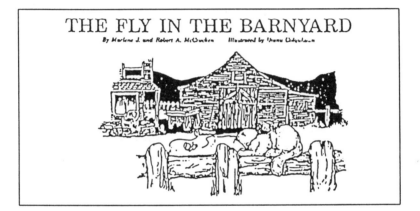

THE FLY IN THE BARNYARD

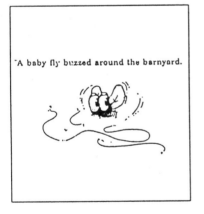

"A baby fly buzzed around the barnyard.

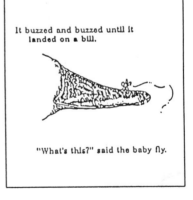

It buzzed and buzzed until it landed on a bill.

"What's this?" said the baby fly.

The Baby Fly

By Cornelius
Genevieve
Jose

A baby fly buzzed around the classroom.

It buzzed and buzzed until it landed on a head.

"What's this?" said the baby fly.

"It's my head," said Cornelius. Buzz off!

It buzzed and buzzed, until it landed on a nose.

"What's this?" said the baby fly.

"It's my nose," said Genevieve. Buzz off!

It buzzed and buzzed, until it landed on a shoe.

"What's this?" said the baby fly.

It's my shoe. said Jose. Buzz off.

It buzzed and buzzed until it landed on a hand.

"What's this?" said
the baby fly.

"It's my hand," said
Mrs. Forsell. She
spanked him, and
he went outside.

Information Books

We must read to children from what we have labeled information books. These are books that are filled with information and usually do not have a story plot. They are the life-cycle books of a seed or an animal. They are the descriptive books of a day on the farm, the city at night, the workmen who keep the city functioning, and so on. These books frequently use vocabulary that may seem too adult, but this adult usage is necessary if children's vocabulary is to grow. The length of information books and their mature language make them difficult to memorize. We use these books to develop vocabulary, facts, and concepts. We have found that some information books become children's favorites, which they demand be read again and again.

The following are superb books that typify what we mean by an information book:

Antarctica by Helen Cowcher
Sharks by Russell Freedman
Animal World Series (8 titles) edited by Jane Goodall
Puffin by Deborah King
The Frog, The Squirrel, The Beaver, The Fish, The Fox,
    and *The Spider* by Margaret Lane
Gorilla, Hunted Mammals of the Sea, Rajpur: Last of the

Bengal Tigers and others by Robert McClung
Spider's Dance and *Snail's Spell* by Joanne Ryder
Frogs by Graham Tarrant
• *Pumpkin Pumpkin* by Jeanne Titherington
Night Is Coming by W. Nikola-Lisa
Sun Up and *The Gift of the Tree* by Alvin Tresselt
Would You Rather? by John Burningham
• *Animals Born Alive and Well* and *Chickens Aren't the Only Ones* by Ruth Heller

We have become increasingly aware that children want to learn facts. Somehow, since 1950, with the communication explosion of television and the emphasis in schools on reading and writing skills, we have rendered primary schools almost devoid of content.

Consider; my own grade-one and grade-two report cards had listed as subjects: reading, penmanship, geography, arithmetic, composition, history, art, and music. I cannot recall what content was taught, but I do remember that reading was only a 20-30 minute block of time each day. Someone recently gave us a grade-one syllabus dating from the turn of the century. It suggests even more content than I had in the 1930s. The curriculum included nature study, literature and history, numbers, language, and the arts. Most was presented in an integrated fashion and used the natural surroundings as an integral part of the work.[2]

This digression is not meant as a plea to return to the "good old days." We are not sure they were good, but the examples do illustrate that content then was a central concern of curriculum-makers for primary grades in the good old days, much more important than reading and writing as separately taught skills.

---

[3] For more information, write *OWL Magazine,* 56 The Esplanade 3304, Toronto, ON M5E 1A7 or OWL Publications, 255 Great Arrow Avenue, Buffalo, NY 14207.

Whole Language

Whole language became the "in" term of the 1980s and persists into the 1990s. The word *whole* should be redundant because language is whole or it isn't language. The redundancy of *whole* is a result of our failing to remember what language is. We have a tendency in education to find solutions to our problems by affixing new labels, presuming that we can eliminate the problem by no longer using the old name. (As an example, I have not attended a planning meeting for over twenty years. They have all been replaced by pre-planning meetings. In its literal sense pre-planning, *doing whatever you do before you plan*, is an apt term, because nothing useful transpires in most pre-planning sessions.) *Whole language* was probably a needed term because in the teaching of language, reading, and writing, we seemed to have forgotten what language is. We need to define language and to recognize the wholeness of language.

To exist, language must

- have a form
- represent meanings, messages, ideas, or concepts
- be used for a purpose, to think, to record, to communicate.

Without all three characteristics — *form*, *meaning*, and *purpose* — there is no language.

From this definition, it follows that there are many languages, not just written and spoken languages such as English, Punjabi, Greek, and so on, but music, art, drama, mathematics, architecture, radio, film, television, and so on. Music has its forms — composing, conducting, performing; and dialects — classical, jazz, rock, and so on. Art has its forms — sculpting, painting, jewellery making, each with its dialects — classical, impressionistic, modern and so on. Drama has its forms and dialects, math its algorithms, architecture its lines and faces with its multitude of dialects.

Film and television are peculiar in that they combine several languages into a single, integrated form. Television by its ubiquity is the most powerful, seductive, potentially abusive language collage ever devised. Within a single minute a viewer may hear music and a spoken language and see several art forms, drama, and text. The appeals to the senses, to the emotions, and to the intellect overwhelm the viewer.

Marshall MacLuhan said that the medium was the message. This seems true with television where both the denotative and the connotative messages of language are submerged to the point of obscurity. We have images without explication; neither language to think with nor time to reflect. Politicians no longer practice oratory, twist arms in smoke-filled rooms, and provide patronage. Instead they employ the best of theater with image more important than substance or platform.

Children raised on television are conditioned against text as a form of language. They rarely see adults reading or writing. They have no opportunity to learn about print. They don't know how text works or what it is supposed to do. They don't realize that text allows time for study, reflection, reexamination, or just the play of repetition. Text does not seduce by a jumbled appeal to the senses, nor does it permit inattention. Text requires an overt, directed attention, or nothing happens. *The brain of the illiterate child, raised in a bookless home, totally ignores text. Because brains ignore things that are meaningless, this avoidance is not an overt act of a belligerent child; it is the normal response of a normal child.* At best, television's child responds to a trademark for hamburgers or soft drinks.

To create literate children through holistic teaching, we must recognize the child and the child's state of development, and we must maintain three conditions as we teach:

1. *We must teach content* — some facts and ideas that make sense as an integrated unit of meaning.

2. *We teach skills through the content* using the best and most appropriate ways we know, appealing to all the senses so that every child may gain access to the content. We must teach responsively, fitting the children's learning practices to their abilities and needs, observing their successes or difficulties in planning what to teach further or what to assign as further practicing.

3. *The children must learn content.* In doing so, reading and writing become purposeful activities as the children read to learn, and write to record their learnings.

None of this is easy in a classroom with thirty or more children beginning to read and write. It takes sensitive, efficient teaching with much hard preparatory work as well as strenuous teaching in school.

There is a paradox in language teaching and learning. Children can learn to read and write from almost any content, so that the exact content is irrelevant; however, there must be content or there is no language. The more meaningful the content, the easier it is for children to recognize the content in text form. The importance of meaningful content is sharply illustrated in the works of Sylvia Ashton-Warner (1959; 1963). Without content there is no language. Therefore, teachers must teach content, requiring children to read and write as part of the learning of the content.

We observed two successful beginning literacy teachers who focused most of the year on two esoteric contents: (1) rocks and minerals and (2) automobile engines. We commend neither as particularly appropriate for six-year-old children. Nevertheless, the two succeeded for different reasons. Teacher one was a rockhound and wanted to make everyone a rockhound, which she did for one year. She taught her content seriously with love and enthusiasm using methods appropriate for grade-one children.

Teacher two desperately wanted to learn about automobile engines, and beginning with a full-size engine in the classroom, the class and teacher stripped the engine and rebuilt it; the teacher read voluminously herself, and the children recorded individually all that they learned. There was, again, a teacher very serious about the content she was teaching.

Reading and writing are never the content; they are the skills that emerge as children work with text so that they learn a content. Reading and writing skills are outcomes, the results of having learned something that required reading and writing, while being taught how *to read and write.*

CHILDREN PRACTICE WITH LANGUAGE

Children Participate As We Read to Them

As we read to children, we expect them to pay attention. But we do not expect silence or a non-moving behavior. Body movement and clapping, tapping, and finger snapping are all part of the natural responses to poetry and song, as is joining in orally or commenting aloud, "The wolf's going to get her!" or "Oooh!"

When we read prose we encourage children to join in dramatically with the repeated parts. This is not disruptive, but the same kind of response that Esmeralda made while sitting on a lap at the age of two, three, or four. Children listen intently; sometimes they anticipate being scared, as in Wilhelmina Harper's *Gunniwolf* when the Gunniwolf rises and says "Little Girl, why for you move?" They squeal with fear, sometimes more so the twentieth time they hear the story, because then they are in control and no longer actually frightened.

Drama

We involve children as part of the reading in a type of drama. For example, in *Gunniwolf*, Little Girl walks "pit-pat-pit-pat" into the jungle. We teach children to say that in a staccato whisper while we read the text:

> On she tripped, farther into the jungle, and began picking the pink flowers, all the while singing happily,
> Kum-kwa, khi-wa,
> Kum-kwa, khi-wa.

We all sing as we stoop, pick a flower, put it in the crook of an arm, then pick another and another. We teach the children how to *hunker-cha* as the Gunniwolf runs to catch up to Little Girl. From a sitting position they raise partially from the floor as they thrust their arms up-forward-and-down in a circular grab, all the while chanting, "Hunker-cha, hunker-cha, hunker-cha...."

When we have read and dramatized the story together we review the illustrations. The children retell the story in their own words, chanting the repeated parts exactly. Everyone dramatizes and chants all the parts.

We do the same thing with *The Three Billy Goats Gruff, Caps for Sale, Hattie and the Fox, The Five Chinese Brothers, Dance Away, Lizard's Song* and others. Children all participate as one class while they learn how to act out the story. Later, we have drama time when children in small groups play out their favorite story without supervision or suggestions. This is a practice time for children. The story may be told inaccurately; the dramatization may be different from that practiced by the class. Children must be allowed to practice in their individual ways — ways that are meaningful to them.

We also use drama to teach content. We read to children from a book that is more content than story. For example, we read Helen Cowcher's *Antarctica*, reading the pages that tell about the Emperor penguin. We add a few more details from "The Brave Emperor," in OWL magazine's *The Winter Fun Book*[3] about the laying of an egg, the

---

[3] For more information, write *OWL Magazine,* 56 The Esplanade 3304, Toronto, ON M5E 1A7 or OWL Publications, 255 Great Arrow Avenue, Buffalo, NY 14207.

EGGS

Lots of animals come from eggs,
Some with fins and some with legs,
Some that chatter and some that cheep,
Some that fly and some that creep,
Some that slither and some that run,
Some with feathers and some with none.
Animal eggs can be quite small,
Or just as big as a tennis ball.
The animals here, there's quite a few,
Hatch from eggs and lay them, too!

Author unknown

incubation, the hatching, and so on. We put children into pairs for drama; one is the mother, the other the father. Mother has just laid the egg and transfers it to Father's feet. Father gets his belly-flap over the egg to keep it warm while Mother waddles off to the sea to feed. The cold wind blows, and fathers, waddling carefully, huddle together for warmth. They stand for 62 days and nights until the eggs begin to hatch as mothers return cheeping to find their mates, claim their chicks, and begin feeding. The emaciated fathers struggle to the sea to feed, returning to swap places with the mothers in a cycle of feeding the chick and feeding in the sea.

We use Ruth Kraus's *The Happy Egg* in conjunction with *Chickens Aren't the Only Ones* by Ruth Heller, learning a large number of animals that come from eggs. We memorize the poem *Eggs* (author unknown, poetry poster, M.E.S. Inc.) shown above.

We teach how the animals move, how they peck and rest when hatching, and finally how they crawl, swim, wriggle, and walk as newborns. Each child huddles in an egg and slowly emerges, walking or crawling, or wriggling away as teacher and classmates guess what animal each is portraying.

From *Puffin* by Deborah King we teach the life story of the Atlantic Puffin, in small segments. We read a page or two, and dramatize the searching for a burrow, the laying of the egg, and the hatching. We do the feeding section another day with three children in each group, one the chick, one the father, one the mother. We start during the day with all three huddled in the burrow. As night falls the adults go to the sea and bring back small fish in their bills, depositing them at the burrow door. We augment by teaching from *The Puffins Are Back* by Gail Gibbons and showing the film *Project Puffin* produced by The Audubon Society.

From *Spider's Dance* by Joanne Ryder we read about the hatching of spiders:

> In the bushes
> a silken ball bursts open.
> Tiny spiders scramble
> over tiny spiders
> over tiny spiders.
> They stretch each new long leg,
> so many legs,
> and dance along the branches of the bush.

Two hands clenched make the egg sac. It *bursts* open, and the fingers extend and stretch forming the tiny spiders who scramble over each other and finally walk along the forearm. We do another page another day, until we have a whole book that we can read while children participate.

Art

Art is another major way to teach content. We frequently combine this with drama, so that as we work with penguins we all learn to draw penguins and establish a butcher-paper rookery full of adults and chicks. We commend Mona Brooke's *Drawing with Children* as the best guide we know for teaching children how to draw. It is a system of observation, labeling, and representation, noting shapes, and sizes, and animal features. As teachers use this book they report that their own drawings improve.

We use individual chalkboards and chalk to directly instruct children how to make an oval for the body, a smaller circle for the head, webbed triangular feet, and so on. We do this once, twice, perhaps even three times so that when children draw on paper they each create recognizable penguins. They cut out their penguins and paste them into the rookery. We may try some swimming penguins and get them into the nearby sea. We study the chick, note the body shape is two circles, that the chick is covered with down so that we make the bodies fuzzy rather than smooth, and we paste the finished chicks in the rookery. We may draw menacing skuas overhead or nearby.

Rewriting
There are several ways to rewrite books.

Have children draw their favorite stories and make big books using the exact text of the story. Sharon Schmidt and her children in grade one from Idylwild Elementary School in southern California created their own copy of *Rosie's Walk* (shown on pages 73–77). Sharon drew the backgrounds; the children drew Rosie and the fox.

Rosie the hen went for a walk

across the yard

around the pond

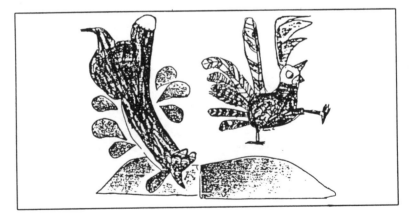

over the haystack

past the mill

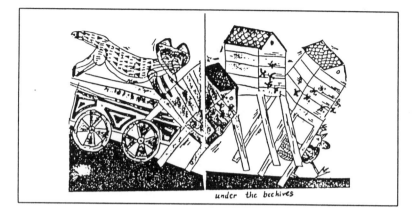

under the beehives

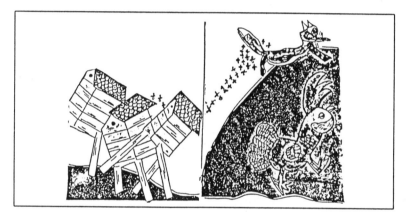

and got back in time for dinner.

Create big books with each child doing a page. *A Hen Can* is a four stanza poem telling what each of four animals can do. The fourth verse is about a fish:

A fish can swim.
He swims in the deep.
He even swims while he's asleep.
He hides in the weeds.
He hides under rocks.
He hides in shadows under docks.
But do you know what a fish can't do?

Carol Berk, a kindergarten teacher in Garden Grove, California had been studying sea life with her kindergarten children. They responded orally to the question in this verse with over fifty suggestions about what a fish can't do. The children were taught how to draw a fish. The children then dictated their personal responses to the sentence frame "But a fish can't _____." The children colored their work, some of which is reproduced opposite in black and white.

Create new versions of stories using the story line of a favorite story. For example in Bernadette Halter's kindergarten class in Garden Grove, California, the children were studying underwater sea life that included a trip to the tide pools. Using *Hattie and the Fox* as their model they created *Hector and the Tiger Shark* (see following pages). The teacher did the background art work with tissue paper and sponge printing. The children worked orally to create the text before dictating the final version. The children did all the art work. One child drew such a good shark that the class decided that he should do all the pictures of Hector, the tiger shark. Another drew such a good sea horse that the class voted to have all the sea horses done by that expert. The other sea creatures were all drawn by different children. Every child in the class could read the completed book. Most paid no serious attention to the words. They did what Esmeraldas do in coming to print: they read the book many times before they learned words.

Ed. note: The wonderful illustrations were not reproducible in black and white. We have traced a few to show the children's style. Here is the story, page by page, with repetitive text abbreviated.

1. Hector was a sea horse. One night in the deep sea he said, "Shiver me timbers! I can see a nose in the seaweed."
2. "Oh rats!" said the sea anemone.
   "Squirt, squirt!" said the sea squirt.
   "Oh no!" said the sea urchin.
   Squish, squish went sea star.
   "Aye, aye, aye!" said the crab.
3. And Hector said, "Shiver me timbers!...a nose and two eyes..."
4. "Oh rats!"...
5. And Hector said, "...a nose, two eyes, and teeth..."
6. "Oh rats!"...
7. "...a nose, two eyes, teeth, and gills..."
8. "Oh rats!"...
9. "...a nose, two eyes, teeth, gills, and three fins..."
10. "Oh rats!"...
11. "...a nose, two eyes, teeth, gills, and seven fins..."
12. "Oh rats!"...
13. "...a nose, two eyes, teeth, gills, seven fins, and a tail in the seaweed! It's a tiger shark! It's a tiger shark!" And he swam as fast as he could and hid under a rock.
14. "Oh rats!"... [except the crab]
15. But the crab pinched the tiger shark's nose and scared him away.
16. And the fish were all happy.

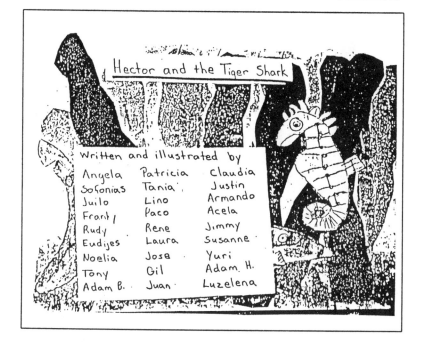

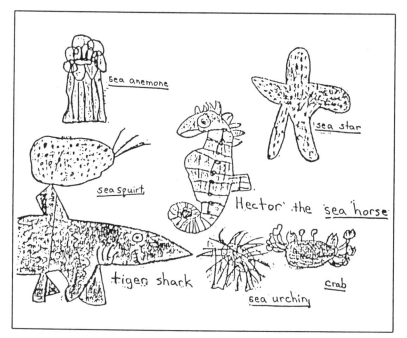

Sustained Silent Reading

Sustained Silent Reading (SSR) is a practice time. To practice, children must know what to do. Telling children to read when they do not know what reading is and do not understand books or how to use them merely frustrates them. Children show this frustration in non-productive, disruptive behavior.

If we are teaching children who have come to school devoid of book language, we delay the use of SSR. We wait until we have filled the children with at least thirty books, giving them time to internalize many of the stories through rereading, chanting, art, and drama. With this base we can begin SSR two or three months into the school year with a good chance of success.

To begin SSR, we put approximately sixty books in the center of the rug. This includes four kinds of books:

1. At least half of the books are books we have worked with. We try to have two or three copies of each of these.

2. We include ten books that are either catalogs or catalog-type books. Richard Scarry's books are mostly catalog books. The Where's Waldo series is a catalog type. We put in toy catalogs and motorcycle or car catalogs and large coffee-table picture books such as the *Encyclopedia of African Animals, Animals of North America,* and *Dinosaurs,* purchased at remainder sales. Children read these books through pictures and mostly ignore the text. Just looking at books and thinking about the pictures are steps of reading.

3. We put in a few books for the Esmeraldas who may be reading independently. These are books we have not read orally to the class, and they may be chapter books usually used in grade two or three.

4. We include class-made books of all types. These are class-created books such as versions of *Rosie's Walk* and *Hector and the Tiger Shark*. But we also include much less elaborate books such as strip books of poetry and songs and strip books of content that the class has recorded

together. Strip books are paper strips with a phrase or sentence from a known song or poem on each page. These are stapled on one end. Ditto paper (8 1/2" x 11" or 20 mm x 27.5 mm) halved the long way works nicely. Sometimes we put a single word such as *Frogs* or *Bears* on the cover and take dictation on ten or twelve pages of facts that children have learned. We put poems, one phrase per page, into strip-book form, using just words, or a combination of words and pictures. Children can recite their favorites and track.

We tell the children to find a book that they want to read and to take it back to the edge of the rug. We tell everyone to read "until I say stop." With primary children, we enforce only one rule always: *No one can change books*. The teacher reads, of course, and ignores noise and sharing that naturally occur.

We expect mostly oral reading from beginners. To beginners, reading silently usually means that no one is listening so that the noise levels in silent and oral reading are virtually the same. We accept that two children may read together, or share and comment to each other. We hope that they may sustain themselves for two minutes on the first try and perhaps work up to ten minutes in the last month or two of the school year.

Some children may want to sustain themselves beyond the time-to-stop announcement. We test this by saying,

"Stop if you want to. Continue reading if you wish. If you want to stop come close to me and I'll read to you." The teacher rereads an old favorite giving Matthew a chance to hear a favorite story again and again.

TAKING DICTATION IN LATE KINDERGARTEN OR BEGINNING GRADE ONE

Much of teaching is modeling. When we write for children just stepping into a literate world, we model many things. We model that speech can be written down and read back. We model letter formation, spacing between words, punctuation, the sequencing of speech, what a word is, and so on. This is not the direct teaching of *how print works*; it is a natural, informal introduction.

When children write or dictate, they must write or dictate about something. Content is central to being able to remember words and sentences, so we begin our writing around a theme. Animals are popular with children, so we often use an *animal theme*.

We teach the entire class about a single animal or a class of animals (reptiles, mammals, sharks, or bears) by showing films, reading books, looking at pictures, classifying pictures, and learning how to draw the animals. Children want to record the information they have learned, so we provide a theme book for each child. The theme book may be cut in the shape of the animal being studied; it may be a scrap book; it may be an exercise book with the top half of each page blank. We like the large scrap book because it usually has more room for drawing and for printing the children's thoughts. With the scrap book we have children draw a line halfway down the page and tell them, "Draw your favorite animal with whiskers in the top half. While your are drawing, think of the two most important things you can tell me about it."

The teacher waits until everyone has begun work before circulating to begin taking dictation. The teacher goes to the children who cannot write for themselves and writes for them. She may help some of the others with their thoughts, but she allows those who can write, to write for themselves if they wish to.

When taking dictation with children who are just learning about print:

- Use the child's natural language. One purpose of taking dictation is to help the child match speech with print. If the teacher does not take the child's natural speech, the child cannot match speech to print. Dictation is a learning time, not a teaching time. The teaching is done prior to the drawing and the dictation.

- Limit print for all children. If children say too much, they cannot remember what they have said to read it back. Ask children to tell the two most important things about their *drawing*.

3

How Print Works

BEGINNING READING

Beginning reading can take a relatively short time span if all of the pre-reading activities and home activities have united to promote literacy. We continue to use many of the same activities from kindergarten pre-reading: art, observation, content teaching, reading-to, and drama. We continue informal teaching, of course, adding formal teaching as we focus on *how print works*. We use many of the same books, stories, and poems that children have memorized, making learning about print as easy as possible. We also begin the formal teaching of phonics, spelling, and handwriting. Spelling is probably the most direct way that children learn how print works. It is discussed in chapter 4.

FORMAL TEACHING OF
HOW PRINT WORKS USING A BIG BOOK

1. Read the story to the children while they watch and listen. (If this is a book all the children have memorized, begin with step 2.)
2. After two or more readings, track the words while reading. The children may join in as they are able.
3. Read and have the children echo.

4. Read together (teacher and children) as you track. (Drop out if the children are reading well.)
5. Have the children read the whole book chorally as you track and listen.
6. Put the story, or a portion of the story, onto phrase cards and have the children rebuild it in the pocket chart. Most children will need help and direction with rebuilding. This may be done as follows:

a. Print the text of the first stanza of a poem or the first few pages of a big book on phrase cards using natural phrasing (we've used the first verse of *A Hen Can* as an example). Distribute the cards, one to a child.

A hen can lay
a big brown egg.
A hen can stand
on just one leg.
A hen can run.
A hen can walk.
A hen can say,
"Bawk...bawk...bawk."
But do you know
what a hen can't do?

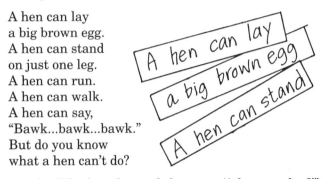

b. Ask, "Who has the card that says 'A hen can lay?'" Take whatever card is proffered and ask the class to check if the card really says *A hen can lay*, helping the children to verify the number of words and checking one or two words through phonics. For example, *lay* begins with /l/, or *hen* begins with /h/.

c. Then ask for the next phrase, "a big brown egg," checking again for the number of words and two or three prominent phonetic clues.

d. As each phrase is added, have the children re-read the text in the pocket chart to predict the next phrase.

e. When the children have rebuilt a story well several times with your help, the cards may be put in an envelope. Put an identifying picture on the envelope and place the set in an activity corner so that the children may practice rebuilding the story independently.

7. Have children practice from big books in sessions that we call *big-book time*.

Big-Book Time

Big-book time, as with SSR, is a practice time. However, it is a much more directed practice than SSR. It is particularly designed to help the Matthews learn about print and to learn what a word is. We use big-book time about three times a week in place of SSR during the nitty-gritty first few months in grade one when most of the children are trying to discover the mysteries of print.

To make it easy for all children, we work with known language by using books that we have already taught. We use our own books in the pocket chart, using pictures first to help children memorize the text. Then we work with the print in the pocket chart, as previously discussed. We practice chorally reading the big book with the entire class many times before asking children to work independently in the following manner.

Have the children work on the floor in groups of a maximum of three, mixed in ability. Try to put one child who knows a little about print in each group. Using two or three memorized unbound big books distribute two or three consecutive pages of a story to each group. Have all three children track the words as they read chorally. We

Children tracking and reading a big book.

give each group a ruler or a dowel (12" to 18" (30 to 45 cm) long); the children grip the pointer, track, and read in unison. Listen to each group as you move around the room. Some teachers call this noisy reading time rather than "big-book time."

When all groups have finished their pages, we sometimes have *performance time*. The children who have the beginning pages stand, hold their pages so that everyone can see, track the words, and read aloud. When the first group has finished, the children who have the next section take a turn. (This practice of reading aloud while tracking is very similar to the practice of "Walking the Walls" that we observed in New Zealand. Children stood with their rulers in hand, chose a section of print on the wall, and tracked the words with their rulers as they read aloud. Children moved around the room reading aloud. Older children held the hands of some recent entrants to help them point as they read together.) When performance time is over the pages of the big-books are put back in sequence and put away.

8. Teachers have had marvelous success creating class big book versions of favorite books using the original text with the children working cooperatively to make new illustrations. Many teachers have found the book *Drawing With Children* by Mona Brookes an excellent guide for teaching children how to draw and illustrate. Mrs. Linda Casper's grade-one class created four indivdual big books, one for each verse. Part of their work is shown opposite. There were many more colorful cows and the book ended with a class picture and the words "A cow can't go to school like you!"

USE OF VERY OWN WORDS (KEY WORDS)

Although *key words* is as much a writing activity as a reading activity, we have chosen to present it here.

The idea of key words originated in New Zealand with the work of Sylvia Ashton-Warner. Ashton-Warner used *organic words,* words with powerful, personal meaning to

[A cow gives milk.]

She eats sweet hay.

[She wanders in the field all day.]

She likes to walk.

She likes to moo.

But - do you know what a cow can't do?

what?

introduce children to print and to relate speech to print. She worked individually with children, writing their key words on cards and allowing each child to keep a personal set. She stressed that words must have personal meaning to be remembered. Ashton-Warner reported good success, especially with Maori children. Ashton-Warner later came to Colorado and attempted to use the key word notion; she reported that American children came to school with lots of words, many more than the Maori children, but they lacked the strength of meaning necessary for the words to be remembered.

We, too, have found that many children come to school without intense meanings for words, so we have worked with six to eight children rather than individually, taking time to develop the meanings of each child's word. We will describe one group of beginning readers in a first lesson with key words that Marlene taught. We call children's own words "very own words" rather than "key words."

Seven children of mixed skill ability sat on the floor in a semi-circle in front of a large chalkboard. The children were told that today they could have their *very own word* to keep. Their word could be the name of something they like, someone that was special to them, some place that was special, an animal, a favorite thing, or something they liked to do. Their word could be anything they wanted. They were given three minutes to think of a very special word.

One of the boys proffered his very own word. He said "Constantinople." All the children said the word *Constantinople* aloud, and they decided it was going to take a long time to print the word on the chalkboard because it sounded like a very long word. The children chanted the letters as the word was written on the chalkboard.

Marlene asked, "Why did you choose Constantinople?" The child explained that his mother had read him a story about it the previous night. He explained his concept of the word. He understood that it was a city far away. Marlene added some ideas and drew the shapes of a few eastern dome-shaped buildings on the chalkboard. The class talked about the way people dressed in Constantinople. Everyone agreed it would be a wonderful place to visit.

The next word was *Boy Scouts of America.* The class chanted it and had to figure out that it was four words. Most of the children thought it was one word. Marlene spelled each word as it was written on the chalkboard and then the class spent a good deal of time sharing ideas about the Boy Scouts.

The lesson continued until the following words had been given, discussed, and printed on the chalkboard:

Constantinople
Boy Scouts of America
university
ballerina
gravity
kitten
killer whale

When all the words were on the chalkboard, the children were asked which word was David's? Which word was Lisa's? and so on. The class read all the words before they were written on individual word cards. The group read each word orally and then chorally spelled it as Marlene wrote it on a word card.

When all the children had a very own word, they took it and illustrated it in their language books. Their job, now, was to write two or three sentences about their word. Dictation was taken from those who could not write independently. Everyone read their story to Marlene and to each other.

Very own words is an exciting and stimulating way to begin children working with print. We use this process along with many other beginning activities. Children like to play with their very own word cards. They read their cards to each other, sometimes trading cards. They take their cards home to read to themselves and to their parents. They create games to play in small groups.

Very own words does not last all year. Children think of exciting, interesting words for two or three months; then their interest dwindles as they are taught how to spell anything they want. They no longer need individual words.

HEARING, SEEING, AND USING LANGUAGE

There are patterns in oral language that are used primarily in speech; there are oral patterns that are almost replicated by written language, and there are patterns used almost exclusively for written language. In kindergarten we work to develop good oral-language patterns and intuitive responses to literary patterns, but we must directly teach so that children learn the patterns commonly used in literature and in non-fiction writing.

Patterns

Books are a source of consistent language patterns. Authors can be our best teachers, since their writings can be repeated without change often enough for children to absorb the language. Children imitate and improvise from these patterns as they speak and write.

Books provide patterns of rhythm. *How Do You Say Hello to a Ghost?* by the McCrackens emphasizes rhythm:

How do you say hello to a ghost,
Hello to a ghost, hello to a ghost,
How do you say hello to a ghost,
If you meet one in the hallway?

Dance Away by George Shannon begins, "Rabbit loved to dance. He danced in the morning. He danced at noon. He danced at night by the light of the moon."

Good Night, Mr. Beetle, by Leland B. Jacobs, recommended for pre-reading chanting, is another poem with a compelling rhythm. "Good night, Mr. Beetle, Good night, Mr. Fly, Good night, Mrs. Ladybug, The moon's in the sky." In fact, most of children's poetry is rhythmic. It is almost impossible to read *Ride* (below) without chanting.

RIDE

by Robert A. McCracken — Illustrated by Diana Colquhoun

Ride a palomino horse.
Ride it to and fro.
Ride it in the wind and rain.
Ride it in the snow.

Ride it in the morning.
Ride it after noon.
Ride it here; ride it there.
Ride it 'neath the moon.

Other books, such as W. Nikola-Lisa's *Night Is Coming,* provide patterns of idiom:

> Night is coming
> Night is coming, and out of the rustle of Grampa's wheat you can hear the whippoorwill's hollow song arising...
>
> Night is coming, and beyond the outline of Grampa's hickory you can see the sun glowing like a jack-o-lantern... Night is coming and out among the wildflowers at the edge of Grampa's farm...

So too does Mirra Ginsburg's *The Chick and the Duckling* provide a pattern of idiom in the repeated "Me too."

> A duckling came out of his shell. "I am out!" he said.
> "Me too," said the chick.
> "I am taking a walk," said the duckling.
> "Me too," said the chick.
> "I am digging a hole," said the duckling.
> "Me too," said the chick.

Books provide patterns of story structure. The story structure may be that of a folk tale, with opening lines such as

> Once upon a time there was a pretty little girl who lived with...
> Once upon a time there were three billy goats who lived near...
> Once upon a time there was a mother pig who had three little pigs...

and endings such as

> ...When the wolf awoke and tried to run away, the stones were so heavy that he fell over dead. And that was the end of him.
> ...As for the mean old troll, he hasn't been seen from that day to this.

...The little pig quickly covered the pot with a big lid, and that was the end of the mean old wolf.

The beginnings are similar, the middles have the similarity of impending tragedy, and the endings get rid of the evil, the bad.

The story structure may be cumulative; *This Is the House That Jack Built*, attributed to Mother Goose, is perhaps the first printed cumulative story.

Each character in *The Judge:An Untrue Tale* by Harve Zemach adds a couplet to a repeated refrain using the cumulative pattern with a story:

A horrible thing is coming this way
Creeping closer day by day.

Its eyes are scary.
Its tail is hairy.

Its paws have claws.
It snaps its jaws...

Shoes from Grampa by Mem Fox is a modern tale using a cumulative pattern for most of its story:

And her sister said,
"I'll get you a sweater when the weather gets wetter,
to go with the blouse with ribbons and bows,
to go with the skirt that won't show the dirt,
to go with the socks from the local shops,
to go with the shoes from Grampa."

The story may be repetitive: Any version of *The Little Red Hen* has a repeated part featuring at least three lazy farm animals:

"Not I!" said the cat.
"Not I!" said the dog.
"Not I!" said the pig.
So the Little Red Hen did it all by herself.

Mem Fox uses a repeated five lines within a cumulative story in *Hattie and the Fox*:

"Good grief!" said the goose.
"Well, well!" said the pig.
"Who cares!" said the sheep.
"So what!" said the horse.
"What next!" said the cow.

The story may be circular: *Rosie's Walk* by Pat Hutchins is told in one long sentence as Rosie leaves her hen house and returns after a walk around the barnyard.

Rosie the hen
went for a walk
across the yard
around the pond...
and got back home in time for dinner.

Laura Joffe Numeroff used the circular pattern in *If You Give a Moose a Muffin*. The story begins:

If you give a moose a muffin, he'll want some jam to go with it. So you'll bring out...

And after several delightful moose feeding episodes the story ends, "And chances are...if you give him the jam he'll want a muffin to go with it," allowing the child to turn back to the beginning and start again.

The story may be interlocking with each sentence or page leading inexorably to the next bit of text, as in *The Farmer and the Skunk,* which begins as shown opposite.

Little Fish (page 100) uses pictures to predict the one word of changed text on the next page once the repetitive story pattern is recognized.

by Robert and Marlene McCracken

The skunk sat under the porch. The farmer sat on the porch.

The skunk smelled the farmer. The farmer smelled the skunk.

The skunk saw the farmer. The farmer saw the skunk.

The skunk got on the porch. The farmer got off the porch.

The skunk got off the porch. The farmer got on the table.

Little fish, little fish, what do you see?

I see a tuna but it didn't catch me.

Little fish, little fish, what do you see?

I see a bald eagle but it didn't catch me.

Little fish, little fish, what do you see?

The structure may be a cultural sequence, such as the alphabet, the days of the week, and so on.

Children's Alphabet, pictured in part on page 44, uses alphabetical order with children's names and toys as its story structure.

Animal Rap uses the alphabet chanted in rap rhythm to create rhyming couplets:

A B
C D E
Dog's in the yard.
Cat's up a tree.
F G
H I J
Cows chewing cuds.
Horses eating hay.
K L
M N O
Hens say bawk.
Roosters crow.

P Q
R S T
Ducks in the pond.
Lambs running free.
U V
W X Y
Chicken in the coop.
Piggies in the sty.
Z Z
Z Z Z
(Canada) Night time comes.
We're all in bed.
(U.S.)Goodnight, goodnight,
from you and me.

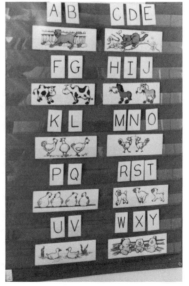

Jerry Pallotta has created a magnificent series of alphabet books filled with bits of content that fascinate child and adult alike. The illustrations are realistic. The first six titles in the series are *The Icky Bug Alphabet Book*, *The Bird Alphabet Book*, *The Ocean Alphabet Book*, *The Flower Alphabet Book*, *The Yucky Reptile Alphabet Book*, and *The Frog Alphabet Book*.

Eric Carle's *The Very Hungry Caterpillar* has become a modern classic. It uses the days of the week and numerical sequence as its structure.

Maurice Sendak uses cultural sequences in three of the four books of his *Nutshell Library*.

Children need to hear patterns

Children need to hear these patterns time after time after time until they are familiar. This familiarity shows when a child intuitively analyzes some part of a story, absorbs the pattern, and predicts what is to happen both in language and in plot. If we begin to read to the class "Once..." the children may join in saying, "upon a time."

> We may begin (from *Where Do You Live?*):
> Do you live in a dog house?
> No! No! No!
> Dogs live in dog houses.
> Do you live in a tree?

and the children respond "No! No! No!" because they have intuitively sensed the language pattern of the story. This sense of language patterns and story structures allows children to predict some of the exact language of a story as they anticipate the plot, listen to stories, and as they begin to read stories.

Children need to see patterns

Children need to see the printed patterns that they already recognize orally. Gradually they see, sense, and learn that writing is *ideas* printed down. Gradually they

Kindergarten classes brainstorm almost every day. Frequently their ideas are recorded on charts so that they may be chanted daily for several weeks, and used in independent language activities.

learn that the conventions of written language are rooted in the patterns of oral language.

Children need to use patterns
Children need to use these patterns in as many ways as possible. They chant, dramatize, sing, dance, clap, improvise variations, and so on to make the patterns their own. The oral use comes first, and the practice is frequently in chorus rather than solo. The children eventually will use their practiced oral patterns in writing, augmenting and varying as they learn to express their ideas.

Sensing Language

This combination of hearing, seeing, and using language fills children with the sounds and structures of the language, with the patterns that enable them to sense intuitively what they must do in writing and reading. As a teacher you must not fear repetition or drill. It is this sense of the familiar, created by the repeated use of language patterns and of individual books and poems over long periods of time (as much as four years) that gives children the security to read, write, and think in their own way. Stories and poems do not suffer from repetition unless they are ill-chosen. Stories and poems, like good silver, gain a *patina* from use that enables each repetition to bring forth a series of responses more mature and better understood than the preceding ones. Words and language are dynamic, ever growing in each child or adult through usage. This dynamic quality keeps language fascinating as we repeat and repeat and repeat.

Much has been said about children sensing language. We are very conscious that this aspect of *sensing* has been a troublesome concept to some teachers. We feel strongly that children intuitively sense language long before they can verbalize or generalize about what they are doing, and long before they can perform on somewhat isolated tests or test-like exercises that purport to measure language understandings. Good teaching, therefore, requires you to have faith in your own choice of teaching activities to develop language, and faith in the learning abilities of children as they participate in those activities.

BASIC TEACHING TECHNIQUES

Brainstorming

One basic technique for teaching language is brainstorming. This is a total class activity. Usually the teacher records the responses on the chalkboard, mainly with pictures in kindergarten, and by words, phrases, or sentences

Right: *Rain* has been brainstormed by classifications: rain in the..., rain on the..., and rain in action. All that remains is for the children to practice their ideas within some structure. This might be poetry, song, chant, or paragraph.

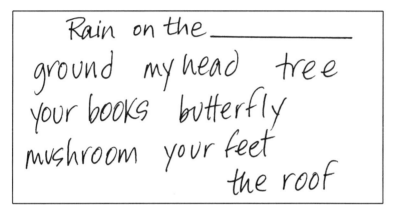

Rain in the _____

cave sky house park clouds
car garage school birdbath
street gutters nest field barn
mudpuddles garden   city
my hood treestump

Rain on the _____

ground   my head   tree
your books butterfly
mushroom   your feet
            the roof

Rain _____

splattering splashing plopping
pouring falling watering
dropping washing gushing
storming dripping running

in higher grades. To brainstorm, choose ideas that you wish to explore with the class. Ask a question and then record answers as the children respond in turn. From the answers you can tell:

- What the children already know (and therefore what they need to be taught).
- How the children express themselves (and therefore how much chanting, singing, talking, and so on may be needed before they write or work independently).
- What kinds of experiences the children have had (and therefore what additional experiences need to be planned).

For example, you might ask:
- "What is red?" and then record in the following ways:

- You might wish to develop a particular vocabulary, so you might ask: "What kind of pigs do you know of?" and then record
fat pigs
black pigs
pink pigs...
- If you wish to ascertain children's prior knowledge or their level of curiosity, you might ask: "What do you know about (Cinderella, the Pink Panther, snakes, and so on)?"
or
"What would you like to know about (Cinderella, the Pink Panther, snakes, and so on)?"

There are three common things that the teacher and children usually do with the ideas recorded:

1. Chant the responses in unison as they are recorded, and in several ways after they are recorded.
2. Copy, or have the children copy, the words or phrases, transferring the language to cards and sentence strips. Then classify and reclassify the information as the children think about the information.
3. Work together orally with the language in the pocket chart, rearranging the ideas as they work with varying structures.

The children then write.

At least one idea from each child *must* be elicited when brainstorming. Forty or more ideas are a desired minimum for a class. This ensures creative, meaningful writing or other output from the pupils. Creativity in writing, drawing, drama, and so on comes from having an enormous number of ideas impinging on the brain.

Anticipating and Predicting Language

Another basic technique is the deletion or omission of single words in sentences or paragraphs. This is similar to the testing technique known as *cloze*. There is a difference, however, in that there is no single correct answer. The purpose of this exercise is to get children thinking and to get them to anticipate and predict the language that authors might use. For example, we might use the following sentence, and brainstorm for words that would fit into the blank spaces:

> It was a_____night with the wind blowing_____through the trees.

Third-grade children brainstorming for ideas to complete a "cloze" as part of their work on an animal theme. The chalkboard is filled with ideas. The intensity of interest can be discerned from the pictures.

We would record many answers for each blank, and then have the children check to see if the words recorded all made sense, and if they sound "right" within the sentence.

Usually, this activity is completed with the oral group work. The children might use the sentence to begin a paragraph for a story. Merely writing the sentence one or more ways is not a thought-provoking task.

Classifying

Classifying was mentioned as an activity that grows from brainstorming. Actually classifying is a basic thinking skill used in concept development. Classifying is putting things together because they are alike, or separating things because they are different; it is linking two or more ideas because they are similar and sorting out the ideas that are dissimilar.

The words that result from brainstorming represent ideas, as do brainstormed phrases or sentences. It is important to recognize that we are working with ideas when we work with words. Children will record information from field trips, walks outside the school, or from books, films, and so on. They will record observations in words, phrases, and sometimes sentences. Together, you and the children will record this information on cards or sentence strips and the ideas are then ready to be classified. A basic direction to the children is to *sort the cards into two piles according to some reason or rule*, then to sort a different way, and then sort still another way. For example, we have the following words when brainstorming what skunks can do:

skunks

spray	sleep
walk	eat
waddle	die
stink	wander
hurry	leap

(Normally, forty or more ideas are needed for classifying to be effective, but ten words suffice for this illustration.) These ideas may be classified in the following ways:

• things seen vs. things not seen
• things that move vs. things that don't move
• things enjoyed vs. things disliked
• everyday happenings vs. rare happenings
• monosyllabic words vs. bisyllabic words
• the past tense regularly formed vs. irregularly formed

The first four classifications are concerned with meaning; the last two with the structure of the words. There are other classifications. We may direct the children how to classify the words if we want to teach a particular skill. Once children have realized what is expected of them in classifying ideas, they work in groups of three to four, to practice classifying, to discover many ways to classify, and to share their diverse ways.

Chanting

Children need to work orally with standard English syntactical forms until they absorb these forms into normal speaking repertoire.

Chanting a poem in chorus needs no explication except to say that children need to chant frequently, repetitively, and with expression that reflects a public performance standard. Chanting from brainstorming needs explication. Chanting several times in one day is not enough. Teachers need to practice chanting from brainstorming in the same way that they would practice a poem. For example, brainstorming in response to the question, "What is red?" we would record using the single frame, "_____ is red." Each child gives at least one response and the class chants the entire chart as each word is added.

To expand on this activity, have each child select a different idea from the chalkboard and illustrate it on a 3" x 5" (7.5 cm x 12.5 cm) card. The children then recite their pictures within the frame sentence "(A ball) is red" and the class chants along. You may put a sentence strip in the pocket chart that says "_____ is red," and the children each place their picture in the blank as the class chants.

Language usage may be developed by chanting the brainstormed chart. We may need to use *a, an, the* and possibly *my, some,* or *all* and develop chants in the following patterns:

A _____ is red.
An _____ is red.
The _____ is red.
My _____ is red.
Some _____ are red.
All _____ are red.
The _____ are red.

This winter bank has just begun and will have ideas added to it as children think more, read more, and listen to winter poems or stories.

Sentence strip books may also be made. Each child contributes a *red* idea on a sentence strip, drawing the idea. The sentence strips are punched and held together with a dowel and an elastic band (see page 84), and the book is chanted several times on several successive days. Shuffle the pages from time to time so that no sequence is memorized.

The individual card-pictures may be sorted (classified) in the pocket chart and the classifications chanted; or they may be affixed to masking tape and the resulting list hung and chanted.

In all of this the children may chant their ideas many, many times before the materials are put away or put into the Language Center for exclusively independent practice.

4

Spelling

For centuries, adults spelled as well as they could, using the Roman alphabet as they struggled to write English, inventing spellings as they wrote. Standard spelling is a fairly recent notion, growing from the 1755 dictionary of Samuel Johnson. In the 1980s we saw the label *inventive spelling* come into popular acceptance, referring to the attempts of young children to spell. The term has connotations that have caused confusion. Parents do not know why their children should invent something that has already been invented. Teachers are never sure if children's inventive spellings should be corrected.

Esmeralda in grade one has drawn two pictures of dinosaurs, a tyrannosaurus rex and a diplodocus. She has labeled the pictures *tiranosorus reks* and *diplodocus*. She has invented both spellings, using what she knows about letters and words. *Diplodocus* happens to be standard spelling, only because it is spelled the way it sounds. She doesn't know that *diplodocus* is standard spelling. For Esmeralda both spellings are equally correct; neither should be corrected.

We prefer to use the word *temporary* to label Esmeralda's spelling. The word *temporary* is acceptable to Esmeralda's parents because it implies that there will be improvement. *Temporary* implies that we will teach so that the temporary spelling will eventually become standard. We believe in teaching so that temporary spelling is constantly improving; we do not believe in just waiting and encouraging children to do their best. Children need to be taught so that they can understand the alphabetic nature of written English and can learn to spell with relative ease. Children should be able to write and record their ideas with a minimum of frustration.

The two current practices of most schools, (1) teaching weekly spelling lists and (2) expecting perfect spelling — correcting every spelling mistake and having children recopy — are detrimental to many children's learning *how to spell*. Equally detrimental is the practice of telling children that spelling isn't important or doesn't count.

Learning *how to spell* is not the same as learning to spell individual words. Until children learn *how to spell*, it is likely that they will always be poor spellers as they try to memorize letter sequences to learn words. There is a rationale for English spelling, a rationale that is disguised by our use of the twenty-six letter Roman alphabet to spell the forty-plus phonemes of English. This rationale is further obfuscated by spellings created three or four hundred years ago and maintained without regard to changes in speech.

Consider this analogy. Suppose you got a new washing machine, but completely disassembled, just a large basket of parts; nuts, bolts, washers, metal sheets, gauges, gears, belts, wires, and so on. You would need a set of directions so that you could begin to assemble the washing machine. Knowing what a washing machine looks like and what it is supposed to do, and given enough time and a little help with understanding the directions, you could probably assemble the appliance. But, if you had never seen a washing machine and had no directions you would not be able to assemble it.

Children are frequently taught the twenty-six letters and sounds of the alphabet. They are given this basketful of parts, but not the set of directions that tells them how to put them together into words. Knowing that printed words represent real things or ideas is akin to knowing what a washing machine looks like and what it does. Spelling skills are the set of directions that teaches how the letters are put together to make words. Those children who have no experience with print are like the person who has never seen a washing machine.

PHONICS

The skill of spelling requires that children learn and apply phonics.

Phonics is a tool of the writer. We teach phonics so that children learn to spell. As children learn to spell, the phonics they learn transfers to reading. To spell with ease children need to understand and apply two generalizations:

1. *Children need to know that when they say a sound, they write a letter.* This relationship between the sounds of speech and the symbols used to record the speech sounds is not obvious to most children. To keep this relationship simple, at the beginning of the child's learning, we teach children a one-to-one relationship between the sounds they speak and the letters they write. More complex sound symbol relationships are learned after the children understand the alphabetic nature of the English language.

2. *Children need to know that the letters should be written in the sequence in which they are said.* This is from left to right in written English.

When children have learned the one-to-one relationship and the sequencing of sounds, they will have grasped the alphabetic principle of our English writing system and then should be able to spell anything they want to say. Their spellings will not always be standard spelling, but the children will have a base on which to learn the patterns of English orthography so that standard spelling may evolve.

For example, grade-one children wrote the stories shown on the following pages in January without any help or copying of words. Both can be read easily. Both indicate that the children *know what a word is* and that they understand the alphabetic principle of writing.

THE PATTERNS OF ENGLISH SPELLING

The alphabetic principle of spelling cannot be learned by merely telling or demonstrating. Children must have repeated teaching and much practice before they can internalize the concept of alphabetic writing.

When children have learned the concept of alphabetic writing, they can be taught the patterns of English spelling. For example, we can teach *ing* as a common ending, or we can teach children that when they say /er/[1] at the end of a word (*remember, tender, September, October,* and so on) it is frequently spelled with the letters *er.*

The English language is besieged with patterns. Most adults are still acquiring some of them. In all probability, patterns will need to be introduced and then reviewed for the child throughout the years of elementary school. We begin teaching the simplest and most commonly used patterns and gradually proceed to the more difficult and rarely used ones.

---

[1] In this book, letters to be read as letters are written in italic, for example, *t.* Letters to be read as the sounds they represent are written as, for example, /t/.

Once ther was a littil
bear and it was very sad
it was sad because it didil
have no one to care
ubat the littil bear it nod
that no boby to care ubat
that littil bear and

it nod no body care ubat it
but then one day a littil
boy came ond said hiyes
said that littil boy that
littil boy said did lic make you
happy said that littil boy
Saib yes it did make my happy.
The End

Chris January 22nd
E.S.L.

MY KITTN

Once upon a time there live a kittn (Wich was my kittin) His name was tabutha. I heared him at my door. So I tooled my Mom. She bring

him in. he was cold, and hungry. We gave him some mete, and we. gave him some milk. Then the nxst day he has

sik. The hole family boked after him. Now he's like a monster. In the morning, When I'm trining to get redy for school. He hides

around kornrs. and then he pounsis on me. and now you know about my kittin.

HOW TO TEACH SPELLING

Kindergarten

Ronald L. Cramer states the needs of early writers and readers as follows.

<u>Six Experiences That Make</u>
<u>Early Reading and Writing Possible</u>

1. Literary exposure at home, preschool, and school
2. Experiences with stories, storytelling, nursery rhymes, and language play
3. Exposure to print and oral language in a nurturing, meaning-rich environment
4. Being read aloud to from stories, poems, and nursery rhymes
5. A focus on children's world of meaning
6. Encouragement at home and school — the intangible necessity

Kindergarten children need to be filled with the totality of language. We cannot assume that preschool or family have done this. They need to hear stories, songs, and poetry. They need to work with language, using language in a variety of ways as they explore the world of literature and observe the world about them. They need to hear the finest of children's literature and the modeling of speech as the teacher teaches them through literature, observations, and experiments while filling the children with the vocabulary and oral structures needed to discuss and record their learnings.

Children need to retell stories in their own words, to dramatize their understanding of these stories, and to illustrate them in many different ways. Kindergarten children need to sing and chant every day. They need to hear language, see language, and use language. *We believe that children come to the act of reading and writing with more ease, joy, and success when the teacher has spent the kin-*

dergarten year filling them with language in as many ways as possible. Reading, writing, and spelling readiness are the years of listening to the sounds and meanings of written language.

The kindergarten program is primarily oral language development with the emphasis upon content. We work orally and visually to get children to recognize what a word is. We track as we read big books, poetry posters, and from text in the pocket chart. When children have memorized a story or poem, they are invited to track words and to match repeated phrases or words. The children are invited to play with text cards as a matter of choice, but they are not required to. All of the print manipulation, tracking, and matching are informal and the children's participation is voluntary. What might be termed formal phonics begins in grade one.

Grades One Through Three

Phonics instruction starts at the beginning of grade one, and continues throughout the year as children are taught how to spell. It begins as an isolated daily skill lesson, but within a very short time, phonics is being practiced in daily writing activities. These daily writing activities are not isolated from meaning because children are recording what they have learned.

We begin to teach what is easiest for the child. Consonants come first because one sound frequently is represented by one letter in standard spelling. Also, consonants are kinesthetic; they can be felt within the mouth because they stop the flow of air. (Vowels, whether long or short, get lost within the mouth; children do not feel them. Spelling vowel sounds can be complicated; many are represented by two or more letters, and the same vowel sound may be represented by ten or more spellings. For example, the sound we call long /a/ may be spelled in a variety of ways: *day, sleigh, date, wait, croquet, cafe, rein, reign, campaign, champagne*, and so on.)

We teach the children five or six consonants before we teach a vowel. With each letter we teach four things within a single lesson:

1. the name of the letter
2. the sound the letter represents
3. the way the phoneme is made within the mouth (the way it feels)
4. how to write the letter (the penmanship)

We have taught *m, b, f, s, t,* and *c* successfully as the first six consonants. These consonants are used frequently and they are made quite differently within the mouth. Except for these two guides, the selection is arbitrary.

It should be mentioned that we can discern no "right" way to teach phonics. We are aware of the problems that isolating consonant sounds might cause; but we are also aware of the dangers of not doing so, and the problems encountered if all consonant sounds are combined with vowel sounds. The secret seems to lie in having children put letters or sounds together to form words as quickly as possible, so that the isolation is momentary. Isolation is used as a brief beginning device to get children to feel the consonants within the spoken language and to understand the relationship between speech and print. The sounds are used immediately within words and are practiced thereafter as children write.

The First Phonics Lessons

As the first step in teaching the alphabetic principle, children are provided with 12" x 18" (30 cm x 45 cm) chalkboards on which they learn to write the letter as they say its name and the sound it represents. *Children need to know that when they say a sound, they write a letter.*

We have found that getting children to feel the sound is the best way for Matthews to learn letters and their sounds. It works equally well with all children so we emphasize *how* the letter is made within the mouth. For example, when we teach the letter *m,* we teach its name, the sound it represents, and how to write it. We have the children say /m/, while concentrating on what they do with their lips. As children say sounds, we get them to describe what they do with their mouths, lips, teeth, tongues, and throats, that they use in making each particular sound. The description must make sense to them. We do not use technical terms.

Next, we play a game, saying:

"Children, I am going to say a word. You must say the word after me. Some words will have /m/ in them. If you say /m/, you write an *m* on your chalkboards. *Mountain.*"
(The children say "mountain.")
"Did you put your two lips together?
Say it again if you need to."

We make sure all the children write *m* on their chalkboards. We dictate four to eight words, some with /m/, some without. The children write *m* each time a word has /m/ in it.

The next day we introduce the second step in the skill of spelling: *developing the understanding that spelling requires the sequencing of the sounds within a word.* To begin this skill:

a) The child divides a chalkboard into four equal rectangles and puts two short lines in each. For example

1 ___ ___	2 ___ ___
3 ___ ___	4 ___ ___

b) The teacher dictates words that begin or end with /m/. The teacher dictates *marvelous, jam, monster, gram,* and so on. The child says the word and puts the letter *m* on the beginning or ending line.

When a word is dictated, the children repeat the word. The repetition by the children is a "must," so that they begin to feel and record their own speech. Each word that is dictated begins or ends with a particular sound, for instance, /m/. The children are taught to write the letter for the sound — *m* — in the first space if they say an /m/ at the beginning of the word, or to write *m* in the last space if they say /m/ at the end of the word. Four to eight words are dictated one day. For years, we tried to teach one letter until the children mastered it. We have discovered that our Matthews cannot learn the first letter until we have taught them fifteen or twenty letters. They need many letters before they can learn how letters go together to form words. We now rarely spend more than two days teaching any one letter. Of course, every letter we teach is reviewed day after day as children use it in combination with all the new letters. We have sometimes found it necessary to go back to the first letter and review the teaching after our Matthews have been taught most of the letters and are beginning to discover *how print works.*

By the third day, a second letter is taught. Each new letter is developed in the same way — saying and feeling the sound, writing the letter alone, and writing the letter as it is heard in words. As new sounds are added, both the old and the new sounds are practiced daily on the chalkboards. We dictate both monosyllabic and polysyllabic words to introduce the notion that children can spell big words, too. Once six consonants have been introduced, all six consonants are practiced every day by dictating such words as *boat, seem, foam, mitt, surf, moss, team,* and *fib.* In doing this dictation with children writing only the initial and the final consonants, children are practicing and reviewing all the letters that have been taught, and are thereby learning the sound-symbol relationships and the sequencing of letter sounds.

The adding of a vowel cannot be postponed much longer so we teach short /a/ in initial position. We follow the same steps used for teaching a consonant, except that short /a/ does not exist in final position. We dictate *am, at, ask, aspirin,* and so on. We move almost immediately into medial position and dictate many monosyllabic words, which they can now write completely: *fat, bat, sat, cat, mat, Sam, tam, fast, cast, stab*, and so on. Consonant blends are not mentioned as blends; they are merely taught as sound sequences. We find that children handle them quite naturally if the teacher says the word once, has the children repeat the word, and then asks the children what sound they say first (each child says the word as often as necessary to write the first letter), what sound they say next (again, saying the word as often as necessary to write the second letter), what sound they say next, and so on. We challenge children to "have the fastest tongue in town," feeling each letter carefully. As children write the words on the chalkboard, the teacher helps them correct letter sequence and add omitted letters as is necessary. *An integral part of teaching spelling is correcting mistakes as they occur, so that mistakes are not practiced.* In the five-minute dictation period, all mistakes children make are corrected.

With the introduction of the first short vowel, the children's writing on the chalkboards takes on a different form. The children are taught to make four rectangles on their chalkboards:

We dictate four words, saying each word once, and make sure that the children have recorded the word correctly. When all four words have been dictated and corrected, children erase their chalkboards. To erase the words, one child is asked to read one of the words, and all the children find the word on their chalkboards and erase it; then a second child reads one of the remaining three words orally, and all erase it and so on. Children get practice in writing, spelling, and, finally, word identification.

Additional consonants and short vowels are added in the same way. Long vowels are introduced differently and treated as spelling patterns.[2]

The transcript (on the next page) is typical in length and in the kinds of spelling errors made by Matthews in grade one after three to four months of teaching.[3] The paper is from a child labeled as disadvantaged according to federal guidelines of poverty. The writing is in response to oral work within the theme *Myself*, after the children discussed what different parts of their body can do. The sample is one day's writing, before any spelling correction (see Practice, page 127). The italics are ours to indicate the misspellings.

---

[2] A full program is detailed in our book *Spelling Through Phonics* and in a sixty-minute video *Spelling*, featuring Marlene McCracken. The teaching of spelling as described here is a somewhat isolated skill. However, spelling is a writing skill used as part of a communication program in which children are expected to write independently. Children soon spend 40–60 percent of their day in writing activities connected to the content they are learning.

When children are taught to spell, taught how to write, and are required to write every day, they learn to express themselves fluently and in considerable length.

[3] From the grade one Follow-Through class taught by Mrs. Jan Mahaffie in Clear Lake Elementary School, Clear Lake, Washington. Clear Lake was part of the Sedro-Woolley School District, a participant in the Washington Triad Follow-Through Program sponsored through the Center for Teaching and Learning, University of North Dakota.

My legs can *cik* a ball and my legs can do a *daes*
My legs can walk me to the store
My legs can *duve* a *cor* and spot the base
My legs can run home and play with me
My legs can *wolk* me home and play out *baek*
My legs can *jupm rop* and hop
My hands can do some house *wrok*
My hands can *pic* flowers and pretty flowers *to*
My hands can do pretty *patning*
My hands can *bons* a ball and *rit*
My hands can pat a *god* and
My hands can play with my *god*

The child has written twelve sentences using a total of 101 running words. He spaced between words consistently, indicating that he knows what a word is. He has spelled 85 of the running words correctly. He can read his own writing as can any adult with a little practice. Some errors, such as "dog" (*god*), "work" (*wrok*), and "jupm" (*jump*) will be corrected immediately. Although some errors are worrisome, *daes* for "dance" for instance, most of the errors are of reasonably good quality and will not be difficult to correct as teaching progresses.

Teaching Spelling Patterns

Once children have demonstrated by their independent writing that they have sensed the alphabetic principle, they are ready to learn some of the common spelling patterns of written English. We begin with any simple pattern that seems to be interfering with standard spelling and move on to more sophisticated patterns in grades two, three, four, and up. The use of the letter *y* on the end of words such as *candy, milky, silky,* and so on, might be the first one. The use of *s* to represent the plural form is also one of the first taught.

Long vowels are taught as spelling patterns with children learning the most common forms. Common patterns such as *tion* are taught and practiced in grades three and above. They are taught and practiced by the teacher dictating and the children recording. We dictate a different set of *tion* words each day for five days, and then the children search as they read for /shun/ not spelled *tion*. They work together to note any spelling rule that they might form to determine when to use *tion, sion, cean*, and so on. If they cannot discern a rule, they revert to the generalization that /shun/ is most frequently *tion*, but if they want to be sure, they either have to know or look the word up in a dictionary.

In dictating *tion* words the teacher might use the following word list:

notion	motion	transportation
potion	mention	section
notation	demonstration	plantation
promotion	formation	meditation
lotion	information	reflection
premonition	rotation	correction
election	explanation	sensation
prediction	location	condensation

Obviously, while the children are learning *tion* they are practicing syllabic spelling, the letter-sound relationships, and the sequencing of sounds that they have previously learned.

Practice

The key to children's understanding and learning is their ability to apply what they have been taught. To learn to spell, children need to write daily, recording what they want to remember. They write sentences and stories independently and apply their spelling abilities in a meaningful context. When children write independently, they spell as well as they are able to. This poses the problem, *what is correct spelling?*

Spelling dictation in grade two. Eight words, two sets of four, are dictated followed by a sentence using two or more of the words.

Spelling is perhaps the only skill area in which we have traditionally expected children to perform perfectly at levels well beyond what they have been taught. We accept children's first baby talk; we expect children to fall when they are learning to walk; we teach children to add sums to ten, never requiring them to do two column addition or division until we have taught them how to. For some reason, we expect children's first spelling to be correct, and we expect their first writing to be spelled correctly. If children are to learn to spell (not just learn to write words correctly) then they must be allowed to practice what they have been taught, and we must demand and accept spelling that is as correct as can be expected as the children write independently.

The way children spell reflects two things: what they have learned, and what they still need to learn. For example, a grade-one child wants to write, "We went on a picnic and it was a gorgeous day." He spells *gorgeous, grjs.* From the sentence it is perfectly clear that he is saying "gorgeous." He has spelled it well for grade one if he has not yet been taught short vowels. If short vowels have been taught, we would expect the child to use them, spelling *gorgeous* as *gorjus.* In writing *grjs* the child has spelled all the sounds that he has been taught and he has sequenced them properly. He is practicing what he has been taught. If we ask, "Is the child practicing what he has been taught?" and the answer is yes, then there is nothing to correct yet. However, if the same first-grade child wrote that he had a race at the picnic and wrote "I ran fats," we would point to the misspelled word and ask the child to correct it.

As teachers we must hone our observation skills. If a grade-five child writes, "There are nine posishuns on a baseball team," he is either saying, "please teach me how to spell /shun/" or he needs to be reminded how to spell it. Judicious nagging is needed to develop good spelling habits. Children must practice what they have been taught,

Five doozers hang in this second grade classroom, the words are printed on both sides of the cards. There are five similar sets hanging in this classroom so that they are easily seen from anywhere in the room.

and we must observe misspellings to decide what needs to
be taught next to enhance the children's spelling.

A child who writes *hope, cape, came,* and *tune* without
the final *e* needs some teaching and directed practice with
some long vowel patterns. The child who spells *grjs, hsptl,
mtrskl* is ready for some work with vowels. The child who
spells *winde, cande,* and *fune* needs to be taught about the
use of the letter *y* to represent long /e/ at the end of words.
There is no particular order to the lessons. We choose an
obvious error, teach it to several children who seem to need
it, judiciously nag them in their writing, and move on to
the next spelling need when this one has been learned.
Thereafter, we demand correct spelling of that pattern.

The Doozer List

In writing or in speaking there is a small core of words that
are used over and over again. A few are phonetically regular, such as *and, he,* and *it,* and they need no special attention. Most, however, are not spelled as they sound. We
call these words *doozers.* It is impossible to write without
such words as *is, was, does, were, they, because, why, of,
the,* and so on. Children will use these words three or four
hundred times during a school year if they write every day.

Children cannot be allowed to practice common words
wrongly for two or three years. The third grader who has
been allowed to write *thay* for *they* for more than two years
will have learned the misspelling so automatically that
almost no amount of nagging will unlearn it. For this reason we begin a "doozer" list in grade one after children are
comfortable with temporary spelling. This is usually De-
cember or January. We choose five doozers, print them in
large letters on cards, and attach them to a doozer chart
or board. The chart is in a conspicuous place in the classroom, and the child refers to the chart as often as necessary in learning to spell doozers correctly. A misspelled
doozer is always corrected as soon as possible. We find that

teachers and children can remember up to five doozers at one time. When no one in the class has misspelled a doozer for two or three weeks, it is replaced by another.

To summarize, spelling is a skill that develops gradually as a result of teaching and constant practice. As with other skills we should begin teaching simply, and allow and demand that children practice as well as they know how. We teach more and more sophisticated principles and patterns, demanding that children continue to practice what they already know and have been taught, until they have learned how to spell at a reasonable standard.

5

Independent Writing

To write independently, a child needs four things:

- ideas, usually developed thematically
- words, developed in various types of word banks
- the ability to spell
- knowledge of the writing structures of the English language

Ideas and words give children the **what** they need in order to write. But children cannot write with just ideas and words. They need to know **how** to record those ideas and words, **how** to get them down on paper with ease. They need to know *how to spell*; that is, *how to put letters together to form words*. They need to know *how to write the structures* of the English language; that is, *how to connect words into sentences, paragraphs, and stories*.

Children who have been read to thousands of times, and who have been allowed to explore language in many ways usually already understand how letters and words go together to form written language. Esmeraldas have learned this from four to five years of hearing sentences, paragraphs, and stanzas being read to them from folk tales, fairy tales, legends, factual stories, hundreds of poetic and rhythmic forms, short stories, and novels. The Matthews — children who have not had this background — need to be taught so that they may become literate.

STRUCTURES

Lists

The simplest writing structures are simple lists. These are just words with an appropriate heading. Children love bugs, dinosaurs, foods, animals, and so on. We may brainstorm by asking, "What foods do you like?" or "What animals do you know?" We record the list on the chalkboard, chanting the list and pointing to words randomly to increase memory and word recognition. The children can draw their favorite and label it. Their papers are assembled into a class book or into several smaller class books for children to read. We may make a word book, putting *I Like to Eat* on the cover and listing each food name on a separate page. Each page has a picture and the name of the food on it. Children read the book: "I like to eat bananas, hamburgers, carrots, candy, and ice-cream." Children can make similar individual books.

Frame Sentences

A second simple writing structure is what we call frame sentences. These are merely standard sentence speech patterns of oral English; we use them to elicit thinking, to develop oral syntax and rhythm, and to make recording of ideas possible for beginning writers in grade one. In kindergarten, we do lots of chanting from lists using frame sentences; we begin frame sentence writing in first grade when we are formally teaching spelling. Frame sentences are a quick and fairly easy way to start children writing. We use a different frame sentence every day because some children will grasp their first learned frame and write with it seemingly forever if we use a single frame sentence for several days. Frame sentences are speech patterns, and they are constricting so we feel that they should be combined with literary patterns and simple consecutive writing as soon as possible.

Frame sentences are the children's responses to simple questions. Teachers try to get complete sentences as responses. For example:

The question:	The frame response:
What can you see?	I can see (a, an, the)____.
What can you do?	I can _____.
What goes up?	A/An _____ goes up.
What can your legs do?	My legs can _____.

We ask such a question, and then record the individual responses on the chalkboard. The first time this is done, we record the children's names as part of the response. For example:

Juan can see a tree.
Mary can see a dog.
Robyn can see a house (and so on).

We track and have the whole class chant all the responses several times.

By the second or third day, we begin writing *I* in place of the pupils' names, and children begin to record their perceptions and ideas with frame sentences. We proceed in the following manner. We ask: "What did you see on the way to school?" and elicit the patterned responses:

I saw a dog.
I saw a tree.
I saw two motorcycles (and so on).

We do this until there is at least one response from each child recorded in words on the classroom chalkboard. We track and chant the responses with the children.

Each child is now given a chalkboard to record a sentence. We give each child a sentence strip and teach them how to use the strip to draw lines on the chalkboard. Children need fairly large chalkboards, approximately 12" x 18" (30 cm x 45 cm). We help them write by modeling on our chalkboard. We write *I* on our chalkboard and teach the children how to write *I* and position it on the left. We model and teach *saw,* and continue with the *a.* If the child has extreme difficulty, we provide word cards for the child to put on the chalkboard and copy underneath, or we print the words on the child's chalkboard and have the child trace over our print.

Next each child decides what to record. We ask the child to point to the word on the chalkboard, and print it to complete a sentence. Children write as many sentences as they are able. Most children will fill the chalkboard in the first session. We teach them to draw their individual responses if the response they want is not on the chalkboard. Children "read" their sentences to the teacher and to each other. The first sessions might be fairly long, requiring forty minutes or more.

We ask a different question each day, brainstorm, and have the children record on chalkboards for a week or two. We are teaching spelling and letter formation within spelling, and as needed for the different frame sentences. When the children's writing standard is reasonably good we begin writing on strips of unlined paper.

Children share their papers informally as they work. This is a fairly noisy social work time. When all the children have finished, we sit in small groups for a more formal sharing time.

Sometimes the writings are compiled into a class book with a cover and the authors' names. The book is put into the classroom library. Usually each child's set of strips is stapled together and taken home to share with anyone who will listen. We call these little books "strip books."

This kind of activity continues daily. Many children are able to record four or more sentences at one time. They copy from the lists on the chalkboard or they draw a response following the brainstorming to complete the sentence. We encourage them to try to spell as much of any word as they can. Copying will not create independent writers, so we teach them how to write any part of the word that they can spell, and particularly we push for those consonants that we have been teaching in spelling. As teachers we must demand that children apply what has been taught; judicious nagging is part of the art of successful teaching. We teach them to write b____ to indicate a word that begins with /b/, and ____b for a word that ends with /b/, and ____b____ when they feel a /b/ in the middle.

Initial writing is done on the chalkboard and then on unlined paper. We teach how to write on lines so that children are able to succeed when we shift to lined paper in exercise books. We do not like the large newsprint paper commonly used in primary grades for two reasons: (1) newsprint defies erasing so that when a child makes a mistake the paper is terribly smudged or has a hole in it from the attempted erasing, and (2) the space between the lines is far too wide, requiring that the child draw, rather than print, the letters. We get a much higher standard of written work when we use good quality paper with almost adult line spacing, and when we use normal size pencils.

We move children quickly into writing daily in individual exercise books. We call these *language books*. We teach how we want children to enter the date each day, and we teach a content, develop vocabulary, create a word bank on the board, teach a structure for the day, have children practice the structure orally, and finally set the children to writing in their language books. Each language book becomes that child's portfolio. It reflects what has been taught, and it demonstrates what has been learned. Most language books show increasing skills with spurts and plateaus of literacy and occasional regressions. It is an ideal record and obviates the need for testing and other

formal, or informal, evaluation. We find that grade-one
teachers need little more than the language book during
parent conferences for discussing a child's growth and
ability in language.

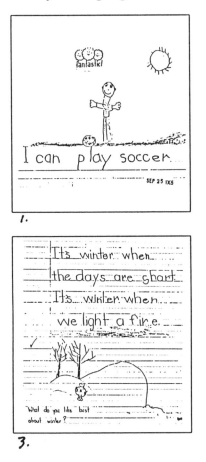

1. fantastic! I can play soccer. SEP 25 IX5

2. They tasted. They were tasty. We read a story about a muffin munching dragon. R

3. Its winter when the days are short. Its winter when we light a fire. What do you like best about winter?

1. The child's first writing was done in the language book on September 25 after fifteen days in grade one. He had been taught how to copy from the chalkboard, the beginnings of spelling introducing six consonants, how to write on lines (which he has not yet fully learned). He will now write daily following teaching, brainstorming, and practicing orally within some pattern before he writes. Stickers are affixed by the children to indicate that they have done their best work.

2. The child left a space to indicate that the word he wanted to use was one he could not even try to spell.

3. The teacher responds only occasionally to the child's writing in the language book. In this instance, the child ignored the question insofar as writing a response.

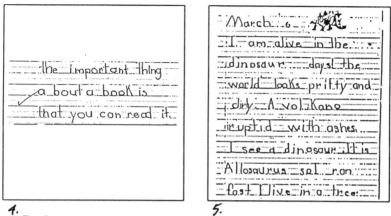

the important thing
about a book is
that you can read it.

March 6

I am alive in the
dinosaur days the
world looks pritty and
dirty. A volkano
irupted with ashes.
I see a dinosaur. It is
A llosauruus sal ron.
fost I live in a three.

4.   **5.**

4. By January the child uses a fairly sophisticated pattern from *The Important Book* by Margaret Wise Brown, now spelling freely rather than copying from the brainstormed answers. The teacher no longer records all of the brainstormed answers, so children are forced to spell if they do not want to use the answers on the chalkboard.

5. By March the child has stopped copying from the chalkboard and spells as well as he can. Note that not even our Esmeralda children are fully certain what a word is (vol kano).

When children have shown reasonable command in directed writing lessons, we add a journal to their daily writing schedule. We use another exercise book for this. We teach them how to date each entry. We generally do not start journals in grade one until the fourth month of school. Matthews still have great difficulty so we develop a frame pattern that they may use if they need to:

Line one: Date
Line two: Tell the weather. (It is _____.)
Line three: Tell one thing you did today.

We encourage freer writing, but some children do not bring enough literacy background to grade one to write daily without this structure.

Las. night I walk Home
when I Home. I Hd. To
lay down

Were you tired?

N-O

9-9-83

01-20-84
Dear teacher
Not lost year but
the year before
the canucks sould
of won the standly
cup but they din't
that was to bad o-well
that year I said
next year the canuck
will win the standly
cup but they din't
so I said next
year. Wouldn't it be great
if they won this year?
Yes I would be happy

01·20·84

Dear teacher
Yesterday what I
don't no what happened
would you tell me
I don't no a single thing
about yesterday was
anybody away expect
me and David was there.
and would mind telling
me about this play.
I don't no anything
like filling me in
about the play tell about it
I'm blanck about yesterday
please fill me in
pretty please tell me
about yesterday I'm cumplete
blanck about yesterday.

Yes I will fill you in, come
and see me immediately!

01·26·84

This boy entered grade one speaking no English, with six weeks left in the school year. He returned in September and was told by his teacher to write in his journal. His first entry reflects what he has been able to learn about writing and English.

He is in a class where children sit six to eight to a table—a classroom in which there is an emphasis upon oral work, and where children talk together at their tables as they work. By January the journal has become a letter-writing vehicle for communicating with his teacher. During this time he has been working with structured writing in a *language book*.

Every day we are still teaching short poetic structures, sentence structures, or narrative structures for short personal stories.

We try to respond in writing to every journal entry. Our responses are communicative to the children's content and thoughts. We rarely make a judicial comment, good or bad. Children know when they have worked hard and when they have not. Their work doesn't always reflect this. Judicial comments, even those of praise, do not really encourage children to think and write. Responsive comments that create a dialog between pupil and teacher seem to work better in generating quality in writing. When children begin to write large amounts daily, it is not always feasible to read and respond every day. We can only say that the more you are able to develop written dialog, the more children sense their own power in their ability to write.

In grade one we begin writing responses in their language books, but since these are directed practice books there is not much chance of developing honest dialog. We want to get children used to reading the thoughts of others, so when Tuan writes [After we have taught about farm animals and have used the frame *Where do _____ sleep?*]:

Horses sleep in barns.
Cows sleep in barns.

We write: I sleep in my bed in my house, Tuan. Where do you sleep?
or: Barns help keep the animals warm.
or: The farmer has to put them in the barn at night.

The written reaction serves many important purposes:

- Children know that the teacher has read and understood what they have written.

- It reinforces the understanding that written communication is important.
- It pushes children into reading writing other than their own.
- It serves as a spelling help.
- Children often begin to write to the teacher so that the writing becomes a prized, personal activity.

We must demand that children do their best as they write, so during part of the writing time we circulate among the children, nagging them to spell as well as they can, ensuring that their penmanship is good, helping them with their punctuation, and making an occasional comment to keep a child working. This must be a sensitive demand. We dare not push children beyond their capabilities, nor must we require that children always do their best. Children have bad days too. There are times when a child's lack of performance should be ignored. Teachers must know their children well, and respond sensitively and wisely to each child. Teachers cannot nag every mistake, nor can they respond every time a child writes. There simply isn't enough time.

Many teachers have found it valuable to set aside ten or fifteen minutes at the end of each morning or day to allow children to share their stories to the rest of the class. This procedure serves many purposes.

- It provides additional reading practice for each student.
- It demands that children listen to and comment on the thoughts of other children.
- It provides the teacher with an opportunity to comment particularly on words or phrases that are used well by children or to teach children empathy by using one child's experience as a basis for discussion.
- It allows all children to feel pride in their accomplishments and in the accomplishments of their classmates, creating a fine feeling of rapport within the classroom.

Some children are reluctant at first to read their stories aloud. We solve this by asking the child's permission to read the story for them. Reading the story, we are careful to point out all the good things possible about the art work, the thoughts, or the words used. Gradually, the child is encouraged to stand beside us as work is shared, and to assist in the sharing by holding the work, reading parts, showing illustrations, and so on, until the child has gained enough confidence in his or her own ability to share work without assistance.

An outgrowth of this sharing period is a "class book." Teachers make a large, fancy book entitled *Our Wonderful Thoughts*. Each day, one or two children who have shared fine thoughts, used particularly interesting words, and so on, are invited to copy their work into the Wonderful Thoughts book, and to add their names to the author's column on the inside of the front cover. This book becomes an addition to the class library when it is filled, and a new book is begun. Many teachers photocopy the material in *Our Wonderful Thoughts* to send home to parents as a classroom newspaper. Such a book can be a strong motivating factor in increasing children's desire to write. Each child should contribute at least once to each publication.

Extending Children's Thinking Using Frame Sentences

Themes or units of thought should provide the basis for much class or group discussion. The language and thoughts are then used to teach children to read and write.

Working with frame sentences is best done following total group discussion related to a theme. Seat the children close to a large chalkboard so that their responses to questions can be written on the chalkboard, then read by children, and used for drill in as many ways as possible.

The following suggestions of simple frames have been used by children in working with the theme "Myself." Each frame should be developed individually.

I can _____.	I see _____.
I can't_____.	I smell _____.
I like _____.	I hear _____.
I have _____.	I taste _____.
I want _____.	I feel _____.
I play _____.	I feel (emotions) _____.
I can go _____.	I can jump _____.
I can run _____.	I can ride _____.
I can walk _____.	I don't like _____.
I can sit _____.	I don't want _____.
I can stand _____.	I don't have _____.
I can hide _____.	Here is _____.
A cat can _____.	This is _____.
Here are _____.	There are _____.

Example Lesson 1

Following a total group discussion where the class has brainstormed for things they "can do," most of the class is supplied with 9" x 12" (22.5 cm x 30 cm) sheets of paper and assigned the task of recording their "can do." Teach the children how to record through examples on the chalkboard; for example, to record "I can ride a bike," write the words *I* and *can,* illustrating the remainder of the thought.

While most of the class is recording in this manner, work in-depth with a small group of six to ten children. Ask each child what he or she "can do" and write the responses on the chalkboard using the child's name in a frame:

Bill can play baseball.
Li Trang can skip.
Fiona can go to school.
Alberto can play football.
Diane can bake a cake.
George can ride a bike.
Daria can play with her dolls.
Ted can watch TV.

As each response is written on the chalkboard, have *all* children chant it. When all responses have been written, have each child reread his or her own response. Then request the children to read one another's responses, saying, "Where does it tell what Li Trang can do? Who can read what Fiona can do? Who can find Bill's name? What can he do?"

Various word recognition drills can then take place such as:

• Children can circle classmate's names as they are pronounced by the teacher.
• Children can underline as many *cans* as possible.
• The phonics that has been taught can be practised; for example, "Can you find a word beginning with *f*? Can you find a word that ends with *f*? Can you find a word with *f* in the middle? Can you find a big word? Can you find a little word?" and so on. Always have children orally read the words they have found.
• Sentence strips can be printed quickly using each child's sentence, For example:

These strips can be cut into words by the children, shuffled, and the sentences rebuilt. Then children can trade sentence strips, telling their neighbors what the sentence should say as they pass their jumbled words to them. The children check their neighbor's work and listen to them read the sentence. The second or third time children do this activity, leave them alone for a few minutes and circulate among the remainder of the class to help them expand their recordings or to offer suggestions of other activities. To expand children's illustrations or writing, ask questions such as:

- Where were you riding your bike?
- What color was your sweater?
- Was it sunny or was it raining?
- What other things do you use to bake a cake?
- Were there any other children with you?

Example Lesson 2

Another type of lesson arises from discussion about what various parts of the body can do; that is, feet, hands, eyes, ears, and so on. Discuss one aspect with the entire class, then allow children to practice a known frame in one of the ways suggested following the sample lessons, while you work with a small group of children.

As before, record children's responses on the chalkboard, but this time substitute the word *I* for each child's name.

The question "What can you do with your feet?" might elicit responses such as:

I can run.
I can walk.
I can hop.
I can skip.
I can jump.
I can dance.
I can pedal my bike.
I can kick.

As children respond to the question, have them demonstrate physically what they are saying. As you write the sentences on the chalkboard, have all the children read each sentence. After all responses have been elicited and written, make the children more aware of the written word by asking the following types of questions:

- Are the sentences the same in any way? Where? How does each begin?
- Which sentence says "I can pedal my bike?" "How do you know?" (clues might be number of words or...)
- Which sentence says "I can hop?" "How do you know?" (clues might be length of word *hop* or phonetic clues or...)

Then point to various sentences and allow individual children to prove they can read by pantomiming the action suggested. Rewrite these sentences on sentence strips while the children watch, or as they dictate them. The strips can be distributed among the class, cut into words by the children, and placed in a pocket chart. All children can then reread the sentences in the pocket chart. (They will probably be placed in a different order than they were on the chalkboard.)

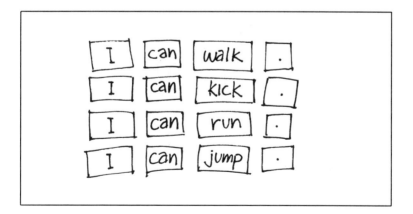

Example Lesson 3

Working with the sentences in the pocket chart provides another thinking-writing lesson. You will need pictures and word cards for this lesson.

Begin by having the children reread the sentences in the pocket chart. Then remove all sentences but one, for example, "I can walk." Ask the question, "What else can walk?" and try to have children respond in full sentences, For example:

> A camel can walk.
> A cat can walk.
> A dog can walk.
> A lion can walk.
> A bird can walk.
> A man can walk.
> A woman can walk.

Create the following pattern in the pocket chart with word cards:

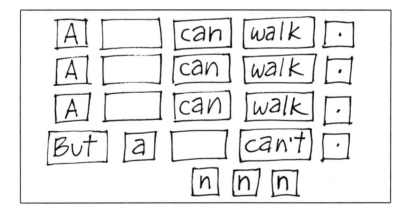

Provide the children with picture cards and ask them to sort these cards into two piles: those illustrating things that can walk and those illustrating things that can't. (Allow discussion and argument between children. This can be done in a whisper — the noise level is up to the teacher.)

When children have completed their sorting, and the piles have been checked for accuracy, have one child from each group put three pictures from the "can walk" pile and one from the "can't" pile to fill in the pocket chart. For example:

Have each child who puts cards in the pocket chart track while the whole class chants.

The children now write on their chalkboards or in their language books using the structure from the pocket chart.

Example Lesson 4

Questions can be introduced by transforming the existing frame sentences. To do this, you will need to have:

- the A card with a capital *A* on one side and a lower case *a* on the other
- the can card with *Can* on one side and *can* on the other
- the punctuation card with a period on one side and a question mark on the other

    "Bill can walk." becomes "Can Bill walk?"
    "A camel can walk." becomes "Can a camel walk?"

Have the children practice transforming the answers into questions and back again to answers. You may wish to begin with two identical questions in the pocket chart, doing the transformations with only the second line after the question has been answered orally.

This should be practiced with many simple sentences, and then all the cards can be placed in the language center for individual work.

Once children have gained reasonable facility with simple frames they should be able to move into more difficult patterns. The teacher can use the more general form of question such as "What can walk?" or "Who can run?" The teacher can ask questions that require a "no" answer such as "Can a camel fly?"

The children will discover they need "can't" and possibly "No" to build:

No, a camel can't fly.

We have found that children enjoy the "No! No! No!" pattern from *What do you have?* or *Where do you live?* to create chants and books. (See pages 54–56)

Example Lesson 5

The most difficult words for children to learn are function or service words that hold little meaning for them. Words such as *in, on, to, from, for, was, were,* and *with* pose a greater problem for first graders than do words such as *astronaut, computer, airplane, castle* and *princess.*

To help children attach meaning to the service words, we suggest teaching them in frame sentences rather than in isolated word drills. This is done by broadening the concept of the key word in each frame. Using the frame, "I can run," discuss the word *run* with children, asking "Where do you run?" Children will respond with such frames as:

I can run to _____.
I can run from _____.
I can run in _____.
I can run on _____.
I can run over _____.
I can run around _____.

"Do you always run by yourself?" will elicit "I can run with _____ ."

Each frame is written on the chalkboard and read by the children, but much practice is needed for mastery of these service words. The next lesson would be devoted to building an understanding and use of one or two service words; for example, "I can run to the store" can be reviewed. Then other endings for the frame "I can run to _____" should be added.

"Do you run anywhere else?"
George can run to school.
Juan can run to the football field.
Sarah can run to her friend's house.
Sam can run to Bill's house.
Moti can run to the park.
Brad can run to Main Street.

These sentences need to be worked with. The children should underline or circle words; then cut sentence strips into words. They need to see that these small linking words that are often slurred in speech are *words* that look different and add different meanings to the verb.

We must be alert to children's understanding of the small differences in meaning made by these words, and must provide much individual and group practice for children in using these words.

The difference between "running in" and "running on" needs to be dealt with.

I run in the park.		I run on the sand.
I run in the hall.	BUT	I run on the grass.
I run in the gym.		I run on the road.
I run in the backyard.		I run on the sidewalk.

Other examples of frames we can use to develop service words are:

- Discussion of the word *like*.
    I like a _____.   I like the _____.
    I like my _____.   I like some _____.
    I like to _____.   I like two _____.

- Discussion of the word *play*.
    I play with _____. I play a _____.
    I play on _____. I play by _____.
    I play in _____. I play at _____.

- Discussion of the word *jump*.
    I can jump on _____.   I can jump into _____.
    I can jump in _____.   I can jump across _____.
    I can jump over _____.   I can jump with _____.

- Discussion of the word *hide*.
    I hide in _____.   I hide inside _____.
    I hide under _____.   I hide over _____.
    I hide beside _____.   I hide with _____.
    I hide behind _____.   I hide on _____.

- Discussion of the word *walk*.
    I walk in _____.   I walk up _____.
    I walk on _____.   I walk down _____.
    I walk to _____.   I walk beside _____.
    I walk from _____.   I walk from ___ to ___.
    I walk with _____.

Extending Children's Thinking
Using Stories, Poems, and Songs as Structures

Stories, poems, and songs all have structures or patterns that children can recognize if they have worked orally often enough with individual pieces. Much of the recognition is intuitive or informal. The oral work in introducing a structure may be done in a single lesson, but usually it is a matter of several, perhaps ten or more, oral workings with the story, poem, or song before the pattern may be freely used by most children.

We want to describe three sets of structures briefly — one story, one poem, and one song. The song, poem, and story are not related in theme. The first set of structures is one that we have used extensively at the beginning primary levels and the second set we have used at the ending primary levels. A more detailed description of individual structures is given in chapter 6 as we talk about teaching from children's books, poems, and song.

Primary Set 1

The first story is the classic *The Little Red Hen*. It lends itself to chanting, particularly the repeated sequence "not I." The sequence is easily put onto a chart and lends itself to sentence-strip and word-card manipulation in the pocket chart. The story is easily dramatized.

At Halloween time *The Little Red Hen* can be used by simply stating that old Mrs. Witch found a pumpkin seed one spring day and asked, "Who will help me plant the seed?" Of course, the characters shift to ghost, goblin, ghoul, and so on. At Thanksgiving the story can be about planting pumpkin seed and baking a pumpkin pie. At no special time, it could be about the building of a swing or playground. These take-offs of *The Little Red Hen* can be done orally first, and then in picture form, building the take-off directly on top of the original in the pocket chart. For some classes, this will be enough. For others, it will be possible to make the take-off into a class book, and still others will be able to make individual books of several versions.

The first poem is *One, Two, Buckle My Shoe*. This is learned orally, and then take-offs can be written. (A late kindergarten introduction of this poem can be found in detail on page 175.) The take-off can fit the theme or season. Two kinds of words are needed to do this take-off. Children will need rhyming words for two, four, six, eight, and ten, and they will need words related to the theme. (We use numerals in the take-offs because the children easily read them and can then focus on the balance of each line.) For example, we might brainstorm for the characters, things, or symbols of a holiday. This can result in the following kinds of verses:

    1-2 ghosts saying boo,
    3-4 goblins at the door.
or
    1-2 turkey in the stew
    3-4 we all can eat more.
or
    1-2 a valentine for you,
    3-4 guess-who cards galore.

Again, these can be built orally, and children can then work with their versions as maturely as they are able.

The first song, *The Farmer in The Dell*, is one of the easiest songs for children to work with. From brainstorming where something might be, the children can make and sing such verses as:

    The ghost is in the air
    The ghost is in the air
    Boo, boo it's scaring you
    The ghost is in the air.

    The turkey's in the oven
    The turkey's in the oven
    Yummy, yummy in my tummy
    The turkey's in the oven.

One way of working with this structure is to record scientific observations about each month or each season in song form. For example, in some areas the following are possible responses to September:

> The leaves have fallen down.
> The leaves are turning brown.
> The leaves are falling down.
> The grass is turning brown.
> The apples are getting ripe.
> School has just begun.

Primary Set 2

No single story is used here, but rather a type of story.

Fairy tales, folk tales, origin tales, legends, and the like all have structures. We can teach children to recognize and write from these structures. The teaching takes two to four weeks before children are fully ready to write their own stories.

1. We begin with an informal review by reading aloud twice a day from the kind of story we want to teach (for example, fairy tales). We read both simple and complex fairy tales for a period of two weeks or more. We collect forty or more fairy-tale books, and during the same two weeks, we assign children reading time in school during which they must read from fairy tales.

2. When we sense that the children have been filled with fairy tales, we brainstorm what makes a fairy tale a fairy tale; we may ask, "What is the recipe for a fairy tale?" We record their responses on the chalkboard. We get a fairly concise, small number of generalized answers from some classes, but get forty or more bits and pieces from others. We take all the answers, put them in sentence strips, and then organize them.

3. We classify the responses in many ways, and then lead the children to organize the responses into basic ingredients and extra ingredients, and then into a sequenced recipe.

We work with whatever recipe the class devises; we are
not looking for a correct recipe, if one indeed exists, but for
a recipe that the children understand and may use as a
structure to write their own fairy tales.

Some of the recipes suggested are:

a. *Once upon a time...*
b. *Someone has a problem...*
c. *They solve the problem...*
d. *They live happily ever after.*
And,
a. *Once upon a time...*
b. *Someone in the royal family has a problem...*
c. *The problem is caused by magic...*
d. *The problem is solved magically...*
e. *They live happily ever after.*

We have had children decide there should be a villain of
some sort who causes the problem.

4. We check the recipe. For this we use the simplest four step
   recipe stated above.

We ask each child to get a favorite fairy tale, and we
check if they all start with *Once upon a time.* Usually most
do, but we put the other beginnings on the chalkboard to
extend the meaning of *Once upon a time*, developing the
notion that fairy tales never happen anywhere special,
always in some unknown faraway place, and always a long
time ago.

We check problems similarly, asking each child to take
a favorite fairy tale and find the sentence or paragraph
that states the problem. We record these problems in
capsule statements on sentence strips. When we have done
this, we put all the problems in the pocket chart and
classify them by the types of problems. For example, the
physical problems (*The Frog Prince*), the magic problems
with spells (*Sleeping Beauty*), monetary problems,
marriage problems, and so forth. Again we work with the
types of problems that our children see.

5. We do the same things with solutions. We may put the children into small groups to share solutions from favorite tales, to record the solutions, and to classify them into types.

6. Usually with the whole class, we select one of the problems and orally compose a story beginning with "Once upon a time." We may create a solution, or choose one of the solutions from the sentence strips and try to make it work. If we can make it work, we end with "happily ever after." If we cannot make it work, we choose another solution. We write two or more stories orally, doing one each day for a week if the children are slow at composing orally.

7. As a last step the children write their own fairy tales. We do one of the following, or a combination of them all. We list them from easiest to hardest:

• Children rewrite their favorite fairy tales.
• We do partner writing; children work in pairs, threes, or fours. They create a fairy tale.
• Individual children write their own.

Any of these writings may take several days.

The following pages show examples of rewriting after this kind of teaching.

Mandy   March 7
There was an old woman and
an old man. The old woman made
a gingerbread boy the gingerbread
boy ran away from the
Littleoldwoman and the little
old man. The woman and the
man said 'stop stop,' but the
gingerbread boy kept on running.
Then the gingerbead boy met a
dog. The dog said 'stop stop
I want to see you.' No said
the gingerbead boy. The ginger
bead boy kept on running.

1.

Mandy   March 8
a Hawaiin Dancer. The
Hawaiin Dancer said stop
stop but the ginger
bead boy kept on running.
Then the ginger bead
boy met a monkey the
monkey said stop stop
but the ginger-bread
boy kept on running. Then
the ginger bead boy met
a gorilla. The gorilla
said, 'stop stop but the ginger
bread boy kept on running.

10.

Mandy   March 8
Then the ginger bead boy
met Jody. Jody said 'stop
stop' but the ginger bead
boy kept on running.
Then the ginger bread
boy met Joanne
Joanne ate the ginger
bread boy. The old woman
was sad because Joanne
ate him.

11.

Mandy is in the upper middle of
her grade-one class. The children had spent three weeks on
The Gingerbread Man — reading several versions, acting out
the story, even baking a gingerbread man. Then they were
asked to rewrite the tale, which
each did using one or two pages,
except Mandy who suddenly discovered she could write. It took
her two days to rewrite the tale,
getting more inventive by the
page, and she only stopped when
the teacher said, "You know,
Mandy, the hardest part of writing a story is ending it."

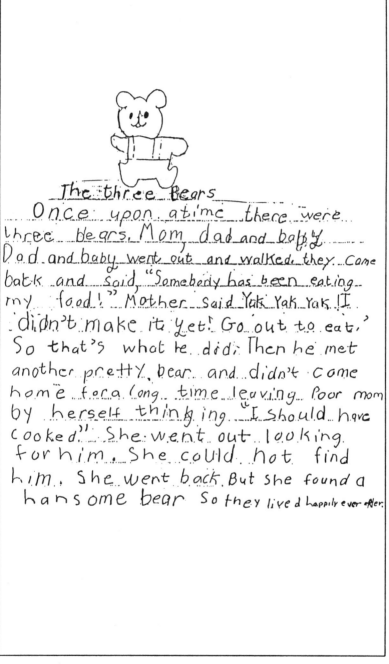

The three Bears

Once upon a time there were three bears. Mom, dad and baby. Dad and baby went out and walked, they come back and said, "Somebody has been eating my food!" Mother said Yak Yak Yak I didn't make it yet! Go out to eat.' So that's what he did. Then he met another pretty bear and didn't come home for a long time leaving Poor mom by herself thinking. "I should have cooked." She went out looking for him. She could not find him. She went back. But she found a hansome bear So they lived happily ever after.

Children bring their own background to their rewritings, as did this grade-two student.

The Prince and The Princesses

Phal is a Cambodian boy (ESL). He wrote this after a month of fairy tales. (+ the brainstorming recipe.)

Written and Illustrated by Phal Chan Grade 2 Sept. 1990

One day a long time ago there was a prince. He lived In a Castle.

A. Princess Came in his Castle.

They be Came in love and they have a baby.

They have 1 baby boy and 2 baby girls. Their names are Marica, Ann and Matt.

One day Ann and Maricar were playing in the garden. The Witch came

and got them. She took them

Phal, with about one year of schooling, is working in a second language. His English is limited, but note how much and how well he is able to do after a month of filling, instruction, storytelling, and being taught how to create a fairy tale. He worked independently (without teacher or peer help) for over four hours to create the book shown on these two pages.

The writing of three other boys in the class (on the next page) is explained in the teacher's Post-it Note to us.

in side her Castle.

Matt came to save them. He had a magic flower. He opened the castle door with his magic flower.

He went in to the castle. He said to the witch, "Give me my two girls or I will kill you!"

He killed the witch and he went to get the two girls.

They started running fast and they got home. They live happily ever after.

Pages 164–166. Partner writing is a powerful way to have children write. For most of September, Bev Atherton taught her grade-three class origin tales using the title *Pourquoi Tales* as a literary theme. As part of this she read from Rudyard Kipling's *Just So Stories*. After, the children, in groups of four, created eight tales. Kipling was reflected in most of these stories. *How The Panda Got Its Coloring* is representative of the tales in the book. They were all equally long.

Pages 167–170. Eight-year-old Danny Wong is a true Esmeralda. He has been in French immersion since kindergarten and now, in grade three, is taken from French one hour a day for transitional instruction into English. The teacher, Mrs. Bev Stout, teaches a literary-type theme during this period. On this occasion, she worked with fairy tales with Danny and his group; however, Danny, in his culminating writing, chose to do science fiction. Although a typist was available if the children wished to have their books typed, Danny choose to print his own on blank paper. The quality of his handwriting is remarkable. (Note he has chosen the Stout Publishing Company in honor of his teacher.)

Pages 171–172. The following year, Danny again worked with Mrs. Stout one hour a day. This year she chose to work with legends and origin stories. When Danny created his book, he made two significant changes: (1) He chose the Wong Publishing Company, and (2) he chose to have it typed (although the typist did not spell the main character's name correctly so he had to correct it).

Pourquoi Tales
by
Mrs. Atherton's
3rd Grade
October 1989

How The Panda Got It's Coloring

by
Lauren Becker
Monica Diaz
Carissa Gough
Melinda Dustin

Long, long ago, in Africa where the grass was tall, there was a beautiful lake surrounded by tall bamboo trees there lived a white bear. This white bear sat with all of her friends, playing and swimming in the lake.

Her name was Panda. She swam, laughed, and played tag with her friends and at noon every day they would sit under a tall bamboo tree and eat lunch and sing songs. At night everyone in the village came to say good night and Pete, the painter, said that everyone thought

she was as beautiful as a snowflake falling from the sky. So she thought she was beautiful too. She was very proud of her beautiful white fur. She always got her own way and was always first to take her turn. One morning Pete, the painter, left for work. He was carrying

buckets of black paint that he was going to use to paint some clouds black so they could have some rain. Pete, the painter, tripped over his ladder, fell in the road and splattered paint all over. Unfortunately, beautiful white Panda was walking behind Pete.

She slipped and fell in the paint. "Oh, no! My beautiful white coat," she cried. She ran home crying all of the way. She burst through the door, wailing at the top of her lungs and rubbing her eyes.

She dragged herself to the bathtub, turned on the water and scrubbed and scrubbed until she thought she was clean and beauti again. When she was fluffy and dry, she went to the village and a of panda's friends started laughing and laughing at her

because she did not look the
way she was supposed to. She
started to cry and she
ran into the pack and looked
at her reflection in the pond.
She saw that the black had
not come off of her ears and
eyes and parts of her body. The

more she looked, the more
she decided that even though
she was different, she was
still beautiful. She went back
to the village and said
to her friends, "If you
think that I am not beautiful, I will go away." They still

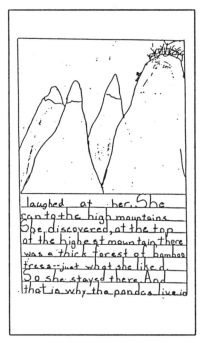

laughed at her. She
ran to the high mountains.
She discovered, at the top
of the highest mountain, there
was a thick forest of bamboo
trees--just what she liked.
So she stayed there. And
that is why the pandas live in

the high mountains and why the
pandas are black and white.

The   Dragon
From   The
Time Corridor

Written And
Illustrated
By
Danny Wong

Stout Publishing Co.
© 1987

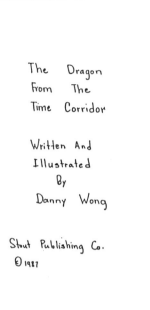

90,000000 years ago, on Hawaii, well, Hawaii wasn't there it was just some Volcano's that were sleeping under the water. Then one day there were giant waves everywhere, then a whirlpool. The water was boiling, steam was coming out of the water. Then lava burst out of the boiling water, more lava burst out from another part of the water, and then another and another. They were Volcanos, they rose higher

1

and higher. When they had finished rising a giant dragon burst out of the lava and went back down.

For over 8,000000 years the volcano's were not inhabited by people. But after that people began to go to this Island, they called it Hawaii. After about 100,000 years there was lots of people on Hawaii, then the volcano's just erupted without any reason. The top of the volcano exploded, a giant dragon

2

3

.burst out of the lava. He could stand the lava, he had a huge horn that could shoot lightning. He had 20 teeth on each side of his mouth, not counting the two giant teeth that were as sharp as dagger's. His stomach was yellow and his back poisonous. His sides were dark green. He had spikes in a row down his back, he could spit spikes as sharp as daggers. On his tail he had a big round ball with spikes

4

.sticking out of it. He had two giant wings on him with spikes on the end. He could breath fire, and red smoke as hot as lava would burst out of his nose if he got mad. His claws were sharp enough to slice a building apart.

Then the dragon flew off and landed in the cities and destroyed them, he ate people and buildings. The dragon said in a deep deep voice, "I have been sleeping for

5

6

millions and millions of years, and now I wake up and find people on earth. Earth is all mine and I have to destroy all these machines and you people so the earth will be all mine.

Tanks came and the American army with their jets and machine guns. The city evacuated to another city and some took the planes to other countries. The army shot their machine guns, their jets dropped

7

bombs and their tanks shot at the dragon. He was totaly indestructable. The army could do nothing. The president of the United States was saying, "Can that dragon really do what everybody says?" His advisers said, "Yes, it is what the people say it is!" "Oh no!" cried the president. "We've got to do something," said the advisers. After two weeks the dragon had demolished all of Hawaii, it sploshed into the

8

water. Helicopters were looking for the great Dragon. They searched all over the oceans for the Dragon but they had no luck. The president of the United States even made submarines go out. The subs found him, he gobbled the submarines up in 3 seconds.

The Dragon arrived at America, he demolished everything. He ate part of the Empire States building and the rest he destroyed. He had destroyed

9

almost all of the countries. He went back to the United States and looked through the skylight of the White House and said, "I have demolished almost all the earth." His voice echoed all around the countryside. The president said, "Kill that thing!"

But the president was so scared he blacked out. The Dragon destroyed the White House and flew to Canada. He started to demolish Canada, he arrived at British Columbia.

10

11

He destroyed Vancouver and Vancouver Island. He went to Delta and it was gone in no time. He was in Surrey, he broke into the Wong's roof and looked inside. Meanwhile scientists were studying the volcano. they noticed that at the bottom of the volcano they could see Dinosaurs. Then one of the scientists yelled, " that's a time corridor, the Dragon came from that time corridor. Another

12

.scientist said, "Then why did he say he had been sleeping for millions of years?" The other said, " Because its true, when he walked into the time corridor he fell asleep, that's what happens when you walk into a time corridor. I read it in a scientist book". The head of the group said, "Get some helicopters out there." The helicopter's destroyed him and they flew to Hawaii. The Dragon

13

followed the helicopters to Hawaii. The Dragon followed the helicopters up to the volcano, they lured him closer and he fell back into the corridor. The people yelled, " Hurray, hurray!" The end!

14

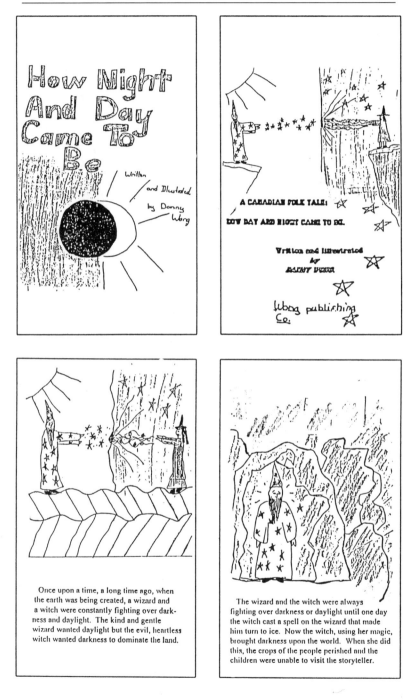

How Night And Day Came To Be

Written and Illustrated by Denny Wong

A CANADIAN FOLK TALE: HOW DAY AND NIGHT CAME TO BE.

Written and illustrated by DANNY WONG

Wong Publishing Co.

Once upon a time, a long time ago, when the earth was being created, a wizard and a witch were constantly fighting over darkness and daylight. The kind and gentle wizard wanted daylight but the evil, heartless witch wanted darkness to dominate the land.

The wizard and the witch were always fighting over darkness or daylight until one day the witch cast a spell on the wizard that made him turn to ice. Now the witch, using her magic, brought darkness upon the world. When she did this, the crops of the people perished and the children were unable to visit the storyteller.

This continue until one day a young boy named Mikituk decided to sneak away from his home to free the wizard. He packed lots of food and provisions and then left to seek the wizard.

For seven days, Mikituk tried to succeed without luck until one day, he found a cave high up in the mountains. He entered the cave and saw the wizard frozen in his steps.

Mikituk started knocking on the ice but it would not break, not even crack. Mikituk cried, "You must save our land or we are going to starve. Please help us." The little boy's warm and gentle tears fell on the ice and the ice started to melt. Soon all the ice was melted and the wizard was free.

When the wizard heard the boy crying, he knew at once what to do. He used his magic powers to cast a spell that would make light and darkness equal. Half the day it would be sunny and the other half of the day, dark. When the witch heard the news, she decided to agree with this but every once in a while the witch gets angry and makes an hour more of darkness when it is supposed to be light. We call this an eclipse.

The second poem and one that has almost instantaneous success is Margaret Wise Brown's *I Like Bugs*. Obviously, if children have brainstormed for any content they can write many take-off versions. The original needs to be built on sentence strips, with word cards, or on a large sheet of paper. In our wall poster below we have substituted pictures of bugs for the word "bugs" throughout so that the structure is blatantly apparent. From *I Like Bugs* children have written as follows:

Black
Green
Bad
Mean
Any Kind of bugs.
I like bugs.
A bug on the sidewalk.
A bug in the grass.
A bug in a rug.
A bug in the glass.
I like
Big bugs
Fat
Shiny
Round bugs
Lady
Buggy
I like bugs.

I like tracks	I like music
Bear tracks	good music
Deer tracks	bad music
Hare tracks	happy music
queer tracks	sad music
I like tracks	I like music
tracks on a fence	music on a sidewalk
tracks in the snow	music on a street
tracks on a rail	music with a rhythm
tracks in a meadow	music with a beat
I like tracks	I like music
thin tracks	rock music
fat tracks	roll music
dog tracks	new music
cat tracks	old music
black tracks	folk music
white tracks	baroque music
I like tracks	I like music

As the second song we have found that the song of the Chicago fire —

One dark night, when we were all in bed,
Old Mrs. O'Leary left a lantern in the shed.
When the cow kicked it over, she winked her eye and said,
"There'll be a hot time in the old town tonight!"

— is a natural for take-off if we combine it with the structure of the Mother Goose rhyme, *Mrs. Mason Bought a Basin*:

Mrs. Mason bought a basin,
Mrs. Tyson said, What a nice'un.
What did it cost? said Mrs. Frost.
Half a crown, said Mrs. Brown.
Did it indeed, said Mrs. Reed,
It did for certain, said Mrs. Burton.
Then Mrs. Nix up to her tricks
Threw the basin on the bricks.

Very quickly the teacher and children can write and sing version 1 below and with a little help transform it into version 2.

1. Ghost, ghost, ghost!
shouted Mrs. Post.
Ghoul, ghoul, ghoul!
screamed Mrs. Pool.
Bat, bat, bat!
yelled Mrs. Pratt.
There'll be trick or treat
In the old town tonight!

2. Ghost, ghost, ghost!
They scare us the most.
Ghoul, ghoul, ghoul!
Beware you silly fool.
Bat, bat, bat!
Diving at your hat.
There'll be Halloween
In the schoolyard tonight!

Versions 1 and 2 lend themselves nicely to a song book with one line boldly printed on the bottom or side of a page and an illustration of the line covering the rest of the page. Obviously, each book can be sung by the whole class as the author turns the pages and leads the singing.

Nursery Rhymes as Structures

One, Two, Buckle My Shoe. The nursery rhyme is chanted until it is known orally. Cards are prepared as shown below and the poem is taught, using a pocket chart.

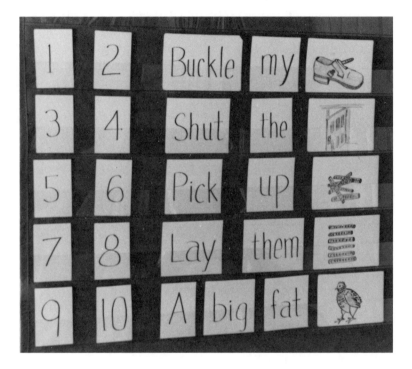

As the children chant, place the *1* and *2* in the chart, and the *3* and *4* as the children get to that part of the chant, continuing until the chant has been finished and all of the numerals are in place. Chant the whole poem again pointing to the numerals as you chant them and to the blank spaces as you say the rest. When the chant is finished, ask if the whole rhyme is in the pocket chart. If the students say "yes," have them chant again while you point to the *1* and then the *2* and then to the blank space that follows as they chant "buckle my shoe." If the students say "no," ask what is missing. When they determine that *buckle my shoe* is missing, ask, "How many words is *'buckle my shoe'*?" When the children determine three words, hold up the three cards for *buckle*, *my*, and *shoe*. Ask which word is *shoe* and ask a child to place the picture of the shoe in the chart.

Next, ask the children if the card is in the right place. To find out, have them chant the first line again while you point to check if the word is in the proper place. Frequently the word is not in the proper place, but the chanting usually helps the children determine where it belongs. (You may have to put it in place.) Ask the children what is missing and orally isolate *buckle* and *my*. Next hold up the two cards and ask the children which word is *buckle*. Then ask children to prove that the card says *buckle*. It is rare, when the whole class is working together, that some child doesn't respond correctly and give one of two reasons: *buckle* is longer or bigger or *buckle* begins with a *b*. If the children do not notice the length, tell them that *buckle* is longer to say and show them by saying it with the children and comparing it orally with *my*, and then show them that one is longer when written than the other.

Work through each line in a like manner, and have the children chant the whole poem again, this time alone, as you point.

Several activities are now possible. (There is no particular sequence for these.)

- Have the children close their eyes, then remove or turn a card over. When they have opened their eyes, have them try to read the chart silently and to tell the missing word.
- Remove two or three words, no more, and have the children replace the words.
- Remove eight to ten of the cards, one at a time, giving each card to a child and making sure that the child can repeat the word represented, and then have the children replace the words. The whole chart is then rechanted to check.
- Say a word and have a child find it in the chart. Then remove it and others, until ten words are removed. Each

child who has removed a word then gives the card to a different child to whom he or she teaches the word and who places the words in the chart.
• To practice and teach the prepositions indicating location, give directions such as:

What word is under buckle?
What word is in front of buckle?
What word is below buckle?
What word is behind buckle?
What word is above shut?

• Prepare a permanent chart with the poem printed as nearly as possible in the same way as the individual word cards. Children can then practice in the learning center by placing the word-cards on top of the poem itself.
• Prepare sentence strips of each line in the same size as the large chart. Place the strips in the learning center for the children to put into sequence either directly on top of the chart or separately.

Many children, particularly Matthews, need lots of work physically manipulating language. Our experience indicates that some 30 to 40 percent of children do not seem to understand how written language functions until they work physically with it through charts, sentence strips, and word cards. This is not just at kindergarten level, but something that needs doing throughout the primary grades. The teacher will need to make charts, sentence strips, and word cards for several books, poems, and songs. For books, the chart can be of a favorite page, or the repeated portion such as "'Not I', said...," or the beginning of the story.

We use picture cards in most of our pocket-chart work even though the children could and indeed do read the words represented without any difficulty. We do this for two main reasons: (1) the children have no difficulty with the words we can picture because they are the words that have the greatest meaning, (2) the pictures frequently recur in visual patterns that emphasize the structure of the written material. (Note the numerals, the words, and the pictures as a visual pattern in *One, Two, Buckle My Shoe*.) This reason is not overly important in one sense, but a stack of shuffled cards containing a few pictures can be immediately recognized by both teacher and children so that some housekeeping and sorting chores are easier.

We have found that the following nursery rhymes lend themselves to similar presentation and to brainstorming for ideas and take-off:

- *A Hunting We Will Go* (Ask children what else they could catch and where they would put it.)
- *Polly Put the Kettle On* (Ask children who else could put the kettle on, replacing Polly with other children's names; what else they could put on; what they would do if they put on certain items.) For example:

Mary put your red hat on.
Juanita put your sweater on.
George put your mittens on.
And go out to play.

- *Ladybug, Ladybug* (Ask children to vary the names and the hiding places.)
- *Little Bo Peep* (Ask children to make numerous pages to show where the sheep might be.) For example:

Are the sheep in the barn?
No, no, no.
Are the sheep in the street?
No, no, no. (and so on)

String Lists and String Poetry

Poetry can be sophisticated, but the beginnings of poetry should be fairly simple. Poetry is just saying something nicely about something.

Children can write poetry easily if they have

- ideas that are related to each other
- words to express the ideas
- some pattern or form
- the skill or the means to write the words

We begin by writing the word *snow* on the chalkboard and drawing a line in front of it. We ask children what kind of snow they know. As they respond, we write their ideas in a list:

<u>white</u> snow
fluffy
cold
drifting

As each word is added the children chant:

white snow
fluffy snow, white snow
cold snow, fluffy snow, white snow

We brainstorm until there are forty words or more. Then we draw a blank after the word *snow* and brainstorm what snow does:

snow <u>falls</u>
drifts
blows
flurries

Again the class gets forty or more words, and again chants as the words are recorded. Next we chant both lists, taking the first word from each list, and then the second:

white snow falls
fluffy snow drifts
cold snow blows
drifting snow flurries

Some word combinations make sense; some won't. Discuss or identify the nonsensical combination. We chant and make more complex combinations. For example:

white, fluffy snow falls and drifts
cold, drifting snow blows and flurries

We record each of the words on a 3" x 8" (7.5 cm x 20 cm) word card (usually two or more children are assigned to this task while the teacher writes on the chalkboard). We put children in groups of three or four, giving each group four cards saying *snow* and eight words from each list, and then ask them to make some phrases using the following pattern:

_____, _____ snow_____
_____, _____ snow_____

We all read and share the results. Then we switch to the following pattern:

_____ snow _____ and _____ (don't forget some *and* cards) and each group writes two or more sentences.

Light snow floats and drifts.
White snow shines and glistens.
Warm snow melts and disappears.

Brainstorm and make lists for

• where the snow falls
• how the snow might fall
• what the children might do in the snow

These phrases are recorded and put onto phrase cards.

You may ask the children to sort the words in each list, telling them to put them into two piles in any way that makes sense to them. We recommend that two or three sets of cards be made if this is to be done with the whole class. When the words are classified, the students who do not know how they were sorted guess the classifications. Eventually, we put the words into some sequence, and affix each word or phrase card onto a long strip of masking tape. We hang the string lists, and now we have string lists from which children can create string poetry.

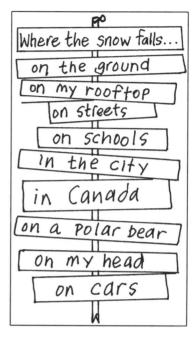

We have hinted about pattern or form. The blank-space phrases or sentences are a type of form. Any pattern that children already know, or any pattern that they can understand easily can serve as a guide for writing. We suggest free patterns rather than tightly structured patterns. We have in some of our other writings suggested haiku as a form. We have come to the conclusion that haiku is a sophisticated form, and that although children can follow it, we get better results when we use it only as a form that says something in ten to fifteen words.

We use other patterns as follows:

• Work with descriptions.
    Tell how snow looks.
    Tell how it feels.
    Tell what you would do in it.
or
    Tell how and where snow is falling.
    Tell how it looks when it first starts to fall.
    Tell how it looks after two hours.
    Tell how it looks the next day.

• Improvise with rhythmic verse.

We have the whole song "Sing a song of six pence, pocketful of rye,..." on a large chart; we sing, dance, or snap our fingers until we are sure everyone knows the song and feels its rhythm. We suggest that we sing a song of snowfall, or snowballs, or drifting snow, or snowmen, and so on. We compose one or two take-off versions orally, record them on the chalkboard, and sing them.

We use the pattern of "1,2 buckle my shoe, 3,4, shut the door," writing, "1, 2, snow in my shoe," or "1, 2, the snow is blue," or "1, 2, the snowballs flew," and so on.

We use the poem *I Like Bugs* by Margaret Wise Brown or *Is Anyone There?* by Mina Lewiton Simon. We use as a pattern any poem or song that the children know or have learned previously.

• Work with couplets or quatrains.

We build these in the pocket chart, shifting the words to demonstrate to children how words may be manipulated. We have the children manipulate the words with word cards. (The physical manipulation of the word cards seems necessary for many children if they are going to be able to respond freely when writing independently.) For example, to change the rhyme scheme of:

White snow snows.
Bright snow blows.
Cold snow drifts.
Powdery snow sifts.

We reorganize the words in the pocket chart as follows:

White snow snows.
Cold snow drifts.
Bright snow blows.
Powdery snow sifts.

We can reorganize by shifting the adjectives; we can reorganize by putting the word *snow* last in each line and asking the children to make the words make sense. We find that they quickly say:

White, snowing snow.
Cold, drifting snow.
Bright, blowing snow.
Powdery, sifting snow.

So we make cards with *ing* affixed, and perhaps another set with *ed* by suggesting that we make the snowstorm yesterday. This forces the children to work irregular verbs, and variations in word endings when adding suffixes. The skills are taught because they are needed in a natural, easy way.

With all of these word strings we can turn the children to creating poetry in any one of their chosen forms. Each of the string lists is a poem in itself. From this oral input and the visual recording children can write easily. We get such poems as:

I wish it would snow
I would play in the snow,
lay in the snow,
jump in the snow,
go plump in the snow.
I wish it would snow.
   — Grade One, January

Drifting snow in the meadow
Sifting snow in the woods
Birds shaking and shivering,
Fluffing their feathers and
Searching for seeds on the
White weed stalks.
   — Grade Two

Is anyone there?
Is anyone there?
Out in the snow?
Shivering or shaking,
Quivering or quaking,
Burrowing or snuggling,
Sleeping or waiting,
While the snow falls gently on the bushes and ground.
— Grade Three

All this creativity results from a single word for which children have lots of meaning, three or four hours of brainstorming over several days, lots of word cards, several string lists, many patterns, and time for the children to create.

Using Children's Books as Writing Patterns

There are hundreds of children's books that lend themselves to brainstorming, discussion, and working with language. In this chapter we detail six stories, and hope that from these, you are able to develop ways to work from *your* favorite books. (Teachers should work from books they genuinely like. Children sense a teacher's love of literature; it is an important message that children can discern.)

Although the books we present are in ascending order — beginning with kindergarten and working to grade three — books have no proper grade level because books are about ideas and ideas have no grade levels. There are, however, levels of maturity in the ways a teacher presents materials, and levels of maturity in the responses of the children. Many ideas worth discussing in kindergarten are worth discussing in grade two or three or at university level. If an idea is worth discussing at only one level, it is probably not very important.

Hattie and the Fox

One way of using *Hattie and the Fox* is to write about content you are teaching using the pattern of Mem Fox's story. In the following example, the content of "the ocean," which has been taught to kindergarten children, is used as subject matter to rewrite the book.

1. Read *Hattie and the Fox* to the children many times, with the children joining in until they are familiar with the content and the structure of the book.

2. Determine that *Hattie and the Fox* has six characters, one a predator. Rewriting the story will require six characters, including a predator. Using the ocean theme will require six characters that live in the sea, so we brainstorm sea animals, recording the responses on the chalkboard.

3. Tell the children that together you are going to try to write a story like *Hattie and the Fox* using the brainstormed list of animals that live in the sea. Ask the children "Which of these sea animals might be Hattie? Which could be the fox?" and so on.

4. Organize the ideas generated by the children, choosing a "fox" and where the "fox" might hide and so on. Then help the children tell a story with the new characters. Next, have children tell other stories aloud, using their words and their ideas. (See chapter 2, pages 81–82.)

5. Have the children write their own stories using their own characters and their own situations. This can be done in many ways.

   • Children may dictate the story to teacher.
   • A class story may be dictated and printed on the chalkboard. This may be copied later and made into an illustrated Big Book.
   • Children may write their own stories.
   • Children may be put into groups of three or four to write partner or group stories.

Brown Bear, Brown Bear, What Do You See?

Bill Martin Jr.'s, *Brown Bear, Brown Bear, What Do You See?* is one of the most popular books for beginners and a must for kindergarten classes. It has a distinct rhythm, a distinct structure, and a repeated rhyme. It is perhaps the blending of these three features of poetry that makes this book a favorite. Before the first reading aloud has been completed, children usually chant *Brown Bear* freely. The story lends itself to immediate extension by having the children add animals or use their own names as they internalize the structure. For example:

> Whole Class: Mary, Mary who do you see?
> Mary: I see Billy looking at me.
> Whole Class: Billy, Billy who do you see?
> Billy: I see Harry looking at me.

1. Teach a content or a theme; for example, the sea or Halloween.

2. Brainstorm for nouns by asking the children a question such as, "What creatures might you find in the sea?" or "What might scare you on Halloween?" Write their responses on the chalkboard.

3. When a group of nouns has been brainstormed, have the children chant each noun aloud, using the structure from *Brown Bear*. For example:

> Ghost, ghost, what do you see?
> I see a goblin looking at me.
> Goblin, goblin what do you see?
> I see a bat looking at me.

4. Print the text on chart paper and have the children draw pictures. Put together to create a Big Book.

To teach children the names of the denizens of the ocean, we used the pattern of *Brown Bear* to create the book, *Little Fish*. (See page 188.)

We build *Little Fish* in the pocket chart as shown. Children manipulate the text as they chant and rechant the story.

Little fish, little fish, what do you see?

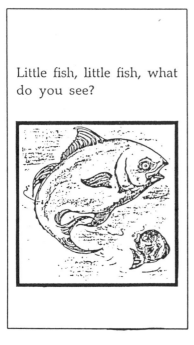

I see a tuna but it didn't catch me.

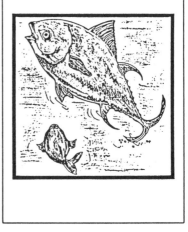

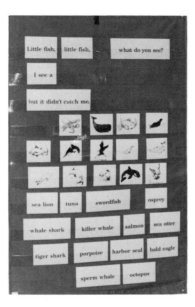

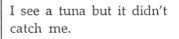

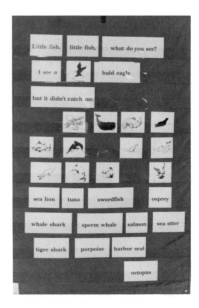

Where Do You Live?

The language patterns in *Where Do You Live?* (next page) are repetitive. The children should be able to sense them and respond during the first reading of the story. (Spend two or more days with this book.)

Day One

1. Read the book to the children and encourage them to join in. Make a word-card strip of "NO! NO! NO!" and place it in the pocket chart. Track it as the children read in unison.

2. Discuss the pictures with the children, teaching them about animal habitats. Have phrase or picture cards of animal habitats to put in the pocket chart. Create sentences with a blank space for the name of the animal. For example:

   A _____ lives in the ocean.
   A _____ lives in the forest.
   A _____ lives on the farm.

3. Distribute pictures of animals and have the children classify the pictures by where the animals live. Next, have the children insert animal pictures in the blank spaces in the sentences. Then track each sentence and lead the children as they chant.

4. When several animals have been classified, use the animal pictures to ask questions such as, "Do squirrels live in a barn?" Chant and track with the children as they answer, "No! No! No! Squirrels live in a tree."

Day Two

1. Prepare sentence cards. A pocket chart with individual word cards works well for this exercise.

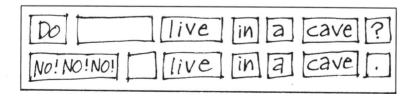

Do you live in a stall?

11

No! No! No!
Horses live in stalls.

12

Do you live in a web?

13

No! No! No!
Spiders live in webs.

14

You might put a picture of a whale in the first blank and ask the children, "Do whales live in a cave?" Move the whale picture to the second blank, and track as the children respond, "No! No! No! Whales live in the ocean."

2. As a variation, add three or four response lines:

[Do] [_____] [live] [in] [a] [cave] [?]
[NO! NO! NO!] [_____] [live] [in] [the] [ocean] [.]
[NO! NO! NO!] [_____] [live] [on] [the] [farm] [.]
[NO! NO! NO!] [_____] [live] [in] [the] [forest] [.]
[NO! NO! NO!] [_____] [live] [in] [the] [grassland] [.]

Choose ten or more animals that live in the ocean, on the farm, in the forest, or in the grassland, and place them in the blank in the first question. Point to the top picture and track the words as everyone reads the question:

"Does a [horse] live in a cave?"

Have one child take the picture and move it to the proper answer sentence:

[NO! NO! NO!] [A] [horse] [lives] [on] [the] [farm].
All the children chant the answer as you or a child tracks.

3. Following this lesson make a class book. Have the children draw pictures of themselves in a cave, a tree, and so on, and ask, "Do you live in a _____?" Have the children answer by drawing an animal that lives in that habitat, and writing, "No! No! No! _____ live in/on a _____."

   A kindergarten class in Great Falls, Montana, created a big book using this pattern. The teacher took dictation. We have reproduced three of their pages on page 192.

4. As a variation, have each child fold a piece of paper into six rectangles, (in half, then in thirds) draw an animal in each left-hand square and its home in the corresponding right-hand square. These are then shared by reading the pictures, "A _____ lives in a _____."

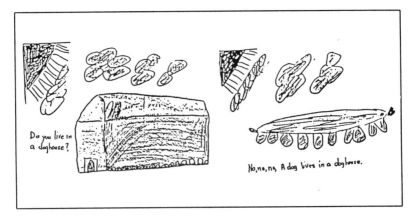

5. To integrate and practice math, do some graphing. Draw appropriate habitat headings on a large sheet of paper, or place picture cards in the top pocket of the pocket chart. Using animal pictures, have the children determine what animals live in each habitat and put the correct pictures beneath the heading. Count the cards and record the findings mathematically and in words as the children read:

   "_____ animals live in trees."
   or
   "_____ animals live in a nest," and so on

6. Use the pattern of *Where Do You Live?* to record children's knowledge of the foods animals eat. For example:

   [Do][you][eat][grass][?]
   [NO! NO! NO!] [_____] [eat] [grass] [.]

7. The pattern of *Where Do You Live?* may also be used to develop other knowledge about animals, such as how animals keep warm. Have the children name different animal coverings they have learned about — feathers, scales, hide, fur, and so on. Divide a large sheet of paper or a bulletin board into sections and label each section with one covering. Have the children cut out magazine pictures of animals or draw animals that fit into each category. These can be pasted under the proper heading. The chart may be used as a room mural and read as the charts in point 5 were read.

If you can, take the children to the zoo to view animal coverings. After the visit, have the children draw their favorite animal, ask it a silly question, and answer the question with the correct response. For example:

"Fish, fish. Do you wear a shirt?
NO! NO! NO! I have scales."

Rosie's Walk

This book helps children understand prepositions (*across, around, over, past, through,* and *under*) and also gives you an opportunity to teach about predator and prey. It will probably be necessary to both define the words and explain the concept.

Teaching From the Story

1. Teach the children *Rosie's Walk* by Pat Hutchins by reading from the book and by using the pocket chart with the story board, picture cards, and phrase cards. (See following pages for photos of one class at work.)

2. Have the children move the pictures of Rosie and the fox around the story board as the story is being told.

3. Place the text in the proper places on the story board, and have the children chant the whole story as you track.

4. To teach the children about prepositions, have them walk around the classroom, past the wastebasket, behind a desk, and so on and get back to their own seat in time to hear a story. The children may do a similar walk across the schoolyard — past the swings, under the monkey bars, and so on.

5. Discuss "chases" children may have seen on television, such as Wile E. Coyote chasing the Road Runner, Tom and Jerry, and so on. To develop the notion of predator and prey ask why the animals are chasing each other. Then ask why Rosie is being followed by the fox. (Some children tell us that the fox wants to play with Rosie, but is too shy to ask. Others have no idea at all.)

   Develop some ideas about which animals eat other animals, and list on the chalkboard other predators who might want to eat Rosie. Also brainstorm what other animals might replace Rosie as a fox's dinner and list these on the chalkboard. Then retell class versions of *Rosie's Walk* using the story board.

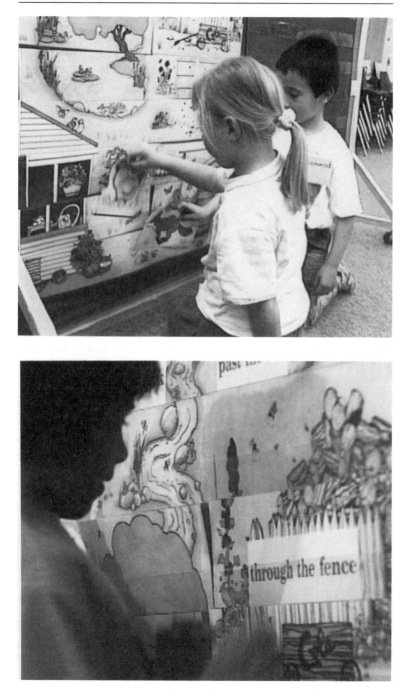

6. Brainstorm other predators and prey and write these on the chalkboard. Then have the children create other walks for other pairs of animals. This may result in a class book or in individual writing.

Cook School in Richmond, B.C. had seventeen home languages in the grade-one class. These children were immersed in English and worked extensively with *Rosie's Walk*. (See bottom photo at left.) As one of their first books, they got a sheet with the phrases from the story to cut out, paste in, and illustrate to make individual copies of *Rosie's Walk*. Three weeks later, after extensive work with the prepositions, they took a personal walk across the school yard, around lots of things in the school yard, over lots of things in the school yard, and so on. Each child then got a booklet the teacher had prepared, with space for a title on page one, and with each of the subsequent pages having only one preposition. The children created various walks for children at their school. Some of their work is shown on page 198. For another rendition of *Rosie's Walk* see pages 199–204.

When we are teaching children to write stories, we compose many versions orally, modeling what might become class books or individual stories before the children start the actual writing.

Jack Nguyen, a grade-one student, is a Vietnamese child in southern California who came to kindergarten with no English. In grade one, *Rosie's Walk* is one of the first books used. Jack decided to write his own version of the book. His illustrations were colored with crayon; his snake began as a green snake, and after the spilled bucket of red paint, his snake was red.

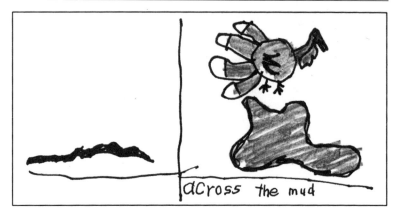

across the mud

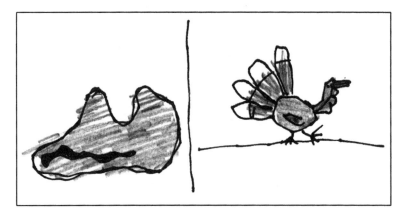

around the fall tree

over the bridge

past the bucket

through the tent

under the table

and got back in time for dinner.

Goodnight, Owl

This book tells of the difference between nocturnal and diurnal animals and the noises different animals make. These concepts will be fascinating to the children.

Teaching From the Story

1. Read *Goodnight, Owl* by Pat Hutchins many times, having children chant the text and make the animal noises.

2. Use the pocket chart with a story board to tell the story beginning with owl alone in the tree. Add each animal in sequence. The photo opposite shows the story board with the owl and many other animals and their noises.

3. Teach children about night or "nocturnal" animals. Read from several books that tell about nocturnal animals, such as raccoons and bats. Using picture cards and word cards, classify nocturnal and diurnal animals. Then, brainstorm night animals, daytime animals, and the noises daytime animals make and list these on the chalkboard as below.

NIGHT ANIMALS	DAY ANIMALS	DAY NOISES
raccoons	cow	moo-moo
skunk	dog	bow-wow
rabbit	duck	quack-quack
owl	rooster	cock-a-doodle-doo
porcupine	horse	neigh-neigh

4. Model a new story with the children, tracking the words from the brainstormed lists, and forming new oral stories. For example:

Raccoon tried to sleep.
The cow mooed, "Moo-moo," and Raccoon tried to sleep.

The dog barked, "Bow-wow," and Raccoon tried to sleep.

5. Personalize the story. Start with the phrase, "I tried to sleep." Have everyone brainstorm noises that might awaken them. (Some teachers have created wonderful versions by suggesting, "Mrs. Jones tried to teach," with the children suggesting all the interruptions of the school day.)

6. Have the class brainstorm activities that require the participant to pay attention, and name disturbances that might interrupt those activities. They might begin:

I tried to read, but _____.
I tried to watch TV, but _____.
I tried to play, but _____.

Our favorite story comes from Marilyn Hrycuk's grade-one class in Cold Lake, Alberta. Using the pattern of *Goodnight, Owl* the children rewrote *The Christmas Story*. It's shown below to page 210.

The children each wrote and illustrated a page, (only some of which are shown here) and then the class grouped to create the ending. The immediate response was that Jesus cried and woke everyone up. This was immediately challenged by one boy who insisted that Baby Jesus was a special baby and never cried. He finally said, "Listen," and proceeded to sing *Away in a Manger*. When he got to the line, "no crying he made," he stopped and said, "See. No crying!" The class conceded and dictated a new ending:

Baby Jesus tried to sleep.

The horses were puffing, puff, puff

And Baby Jesus tried to sleep.

Baby Jesus tried to
sleep the Little
Drummer Boy played
his drum .
A rum pa pum. A rum
And Baby Jes tried to sleep.

Baby Jesus tried to sleep

The angels were blowing

their horns Toot Toot And Baby

Jesus tried to sleep.

Baby Jesus tried to sleep.
The three Kings were
arguing. "I brought the best
present." "No! I brought
And Baby Jesus tried to sleep.

Baby Jesus tried to sleep

The donkeys were hee hawing

Hee haw

And Baby Jes tred to sleep.

— Baby Jesus tried to sleep
— the sheperds talked
— we will show the King.
and Baby Lesus tried to sleep

Baby Jesus tried to sleep.

The camels were stomping.

Bang bang

And Baby Jesus tried to sleep .

Baby Jesus tried   to   sleep   The

star   was   shining In   his   eyes

And   Baby Jesus tried to sleep .

Baby Jesus tried to sleep.

The angels were singing.

Rock-a-my-Babyy.

And Baby Jesus tried to   Sleep.

Baby Jesus tried tosleep.
The hay was prickly
crack, crack
and   Baby Jesus tried tosleep.

Baby   Jesus   tried   to   sleep

the thre   wiseman   talked   to   much

"Baby Jesus   is Born!".

        And Baby   Jesus tried to sleep.

Everybody was getting tired of talking and
 talking.
It was night time and they fell asleep
And there was no noise.
Baby Jesus screamed, "GOO! GOO!"
And woke everybody up.

The Longest Journey in the World

Most books we use are to be read and enjoyed, but we also use some books as teaching tools to develop content, language skills, creativity, and thinking. These types of books take more than one day; *The Longest Journey in the World* by William Barrett Morris takes at least a week (and can be used as part of a Bugs or Insects theme.)

Day One

1. Read *The Longest Journey in the World* orally and show children the pictures. (The illustrations are necessary because they show a caterpillar's view of the world.)

2. Enlarge the text and build it in the pocket chart, using pictures to represent the caterpillar's journey.

3. Track the words as the children read the story chorally.

4. Remove the pictures of the journey from the pocket chart. Shuffle the pictures and distribute them to the children. Have the children try to put the pictures back in the pocket chart in correct sequence. Then read the journey section of the book orally while children watch to see if the sequence in the pocket chart is correct.

5. Distribute the phrase cards that match the pictures. Have the children match text to picture, then have the class read silently to see if all is correct.

6. Remove the pictures, so that only the text of the story remains in the pocket chart.

7. Remove and shuffle all the phrase cards (the entire text of the story) and distribute to the children. To increase memory, apprehension, and comprehension, have children recreate the story. Do this by asking, "Who has the beginning of the story?" Accept all proffered phrase cards. Have children read them aloud and decide which is the beginning. Ask, "Who has the card that comes next?" and have children work their way through the rest of the story. Sometimes you might have to ask, "Does this card make sense?" requiring the children to reread the part of the story already built.

Day Two
1. Read stories and poems to the children about bugs or "creepy crawlers."

2. Brainstorm and make a creepy crawler list on the chalkboard. Chant the list.

3. Have children locate the creepy crawlers on the chalkboard from oral clues. For example:

   What bug is red with black dots?
   What bug might bite you?
   Which of these animals might slither across the grass?

4. Shuffle the text cards, and distribute them to the children to rebuild *The Longest Journey in the World* again.

Day Three
1. Continue reading stories about bugs and add to the list of creepy crawlers.

2. Tell the children, "There were many bugs in the corner of the playground yesterday morning. Last night, they were on the opposite corner of the playground. How did they get there?" Brainstorm how each bug moved across the playground, eliciting verbs in the past tense that describe how each particular bug might have moved. Record these words in a list on the chalkboard next to the creepy crawler list.

3. Brainstorm for prepositional phrases asking, "What might the bugs have scurried over, around, under, near, behind?" and so on. Record this list of phrases on the chalkboard next to the list of verbs.

4. Chant each list.

Day Four

1. Use the bug list, the verb list, and the prepositional phrase list and model a new story using the structure of *The Longest Journey in the World*.

2. Open children's thinking for new ideas. Ask children where bugs might be other than on the playground. Some ideas children have suggested are:

Disneyland
Hawaii
a supermarket
the classroom
a bedroom
a barn, and so on.

3. Have the children choose their favorite creepy crawler and their favorite location, and begin to write a story based on the pattern of *The Longest Journey in the World*.

Day Five

1. Have the children complete their stories.

2. Have the children share their stories with their classmates.

The story shown on pages 215–217 was written by a six-year-old child.

One morning as the sun was coming up, a little ladybug said to himself

I
am
going
on
a
long
journey.

Tanyo

He walked and he walked and he walked. He walked over a big car.

Toy car

He walked across a Giant.

baby

He walked around a large table.

mushroom

USING SONGS TO TELL ABOUT STORIES AND CONTENT

Like it or not, music surrounds us — rap, heavy metal, rock, and country engulf children. Because music is so pervasive we incorporate it into the learning process by teaching children how to use music for writing and for book reporting.

Step 1: Sing a song until every child knows it by memory. (Hopefully, kindergarten children will learn many songs, songs that they may use later in writing activities.)

Step 2: Write the song lyrics on the chalkboard. Better still, write the words on individuals word cards and build the lyrics in the pocket chart. Track while the children sing the song. For example, we take the first line of the song and ask the children what it tells us.

The farmer in the dell is identified as telling us where the farmer is.
One dark night tells us the time.
We create a question that would elicit the answer.
Where is the farmer?
What time is it?

We create several answers to fit the content we are teaching and to fit the context of the classroom to get children to understand how to create the song beginning:

The farmer in the house...
The farmer in the barn...
We are in the school...
We are on the rug...
We are near the window...
And
One fine day...
One cold day...
One Halloween night...and so on.

Step 3: Ask the children how the lyricist put the song together. Note the rhythmic patterns and the way in which the content is expressed.

Step 4: Concurrent with steps 1–3, teach a content. Brainstorm what has been learned and record this where everyone can see the facts. Using sentence strips in the pocket chart is excellent and allows text manipulation.

Step 5: Model how to impose the ideas upon the song pattern. If children grasp the idea quickly, go to the next step. If the children have difficulty, create verses as a class and have groups of children illustrate each verse or line to make a class book.

Step 6: Have the children write songs. (We recommend partner writing for this.)

Step 7: Have the children sing their songs, make cards to put their lyrics in the pocket chart, and lead the class in singing.

Step 8: Compile several of the verses into a sequenced class book.

We have found the following songs work well, as is demonstrated using the plot and facts from *Charlotte's Web* and content from a theme on whales:

My Hat It Has Three Corners
Frère Jacques
The Farmer in the Dell
The Bear Went Over the Mountain
Good Morning to the Sun
Skip to my Loo

Following the pattern of "My Hat It Has Three Corners" closely, we have "composed":

Oh, Charlotte spun "Some pig!"
"Some pig!" Charlotte spun.
And was it not "Some pig!"
It wasn't Charlotte's work.

Oh, Wilbur was a piglet,
A piglet was Wilbur.
And were he not a piglet.
He would not be Wilbur.

Or we might use the content from a study about whales.

The narwhal has a tusk.
A tusk the narwhal has.
And had it not a tusk.
It would not be a narwhal.

Or we can follow the rhythm freely without using the text model:

Zuckerman's fattening Wilbur
To cut him into chops,
But Charlotte wrote, "Some Pig,"
And Wilbur's slaughter stopped.

Following the pattern of "Frère Jacques" we can write
an eight line precis:

Wilbur's worried.
Wilbur's worried.
Butchering time.
Butchering time.
Charlotte writes FANTASTIC.
Charlotte writes FANTASTIC.
Wilbur's fine.
Wilbur's fine.

The whale's are sounding.
The whale's are sounding.
Diving down.
Diving down.
Deep into the waters.
Deep into the waters.
We don't know why.
We don't know why.

Following the pattern of "The Farmer in the Dell" we
can write a three verse summary:

Wilbur's in his pen.
Wilbur's in his pen.
Hoping he won't be slaughtered.
Wilbur's in his pen.

Wilbur's at the fair.
Wilbur's at the fair.
He won a special medal.
Wilbur's at the fair.

Wilbur won't be killed.
Wilbur won't be killed.
Thanks to Charlotte spinning words,
Wilbur won't be killed.

Grey whales migrate south.
Grey whales migrate south.
Heading south to Baja land.
Grey whales migrate south.

The calves are being born.
The calves are being born.
In the warm Baja lagoons,
The calves are being born.

In summer they go north.
In summer they go north.
Right up to the Bering Sea.
In summer they go north.

Following the pattern of "The Bear Went Over the Mountain," we can recount an episode:

Lurvy's slopping Wilbur.
Lurvy's slopping Wilbur.
Lurvy's slopping Wilbur.
Wilbur loves to eat.

The baleen whales eat krill.
The baleen whales eat krill.
The baleen whales eat krill.
They eat both day and night.

Following the pattern of "Good Morning to the Sun" we can review some facts:

I say good morning to the spider,
good morning to the girl,
good morning to the piggie in his pen.
I say good morning to the farmer,
good morning to the hired man,
good morning to the rat in his den.

I say good morning to the right whales,
good morning to the sei whales,
good morning to the blue whales eating krill.
I say good morning to the sperm whales,
good morning to the humpbacks,
good morning to the finbacks lying still.

Following the pattern of "Skip to my Loo" we can use a repeated chorus to recount several episodes:

Slops in the bucket.
Wilbur will be fed.
Slops in the bucket.
Wilbur will be fed.
Slops in the bucket.
Wilbur will be fed.
Lurvy's slopping Wilbur.

Chorus
Slops, slops, slops are coming.
Slops, slops, slops are coming.
Slops, slops, slops are coming.
It's time for Wilbur's breakfast.

Templeton is hiding under the trough.
Templeton is hiding under the trough.
Templeton is hiding under the trough.
Lurvy's slopping Wilbur.

Chorus
Slops, slops, slops are coming.
Slops, slops, slops are coming.
Slops, slops, slops are coming.
It's time for Wilbur's breakfast.

The blue whale weighs
more than a ton.
The blue whale weighs
more than a ton.
The blue whale weighs
more than a ton.
It needs a lot of food.

Chorus
Dive, surface, blow and breathe.
Dive, surface, blow and breathe.
Dive, surface, blow and breathe.
Whales breathe air as we do.

The blue whale's feeding
Eating krill.
The blue whale's feeding
Eating krill.
The blue whale's feeding
Eating krill.
It eats two tons each day.

Chorus
Dive, surface, blow and breathe.
Dive, surface, blow and breathe.
Dive, surface, blow and breathe.
Whales breathe air as we do.

All language consists of patterns; all books are patterned in that they use language. Several book patterns are simple and, therefore, are easily discernable; others are complex, combining several patterns into a collage. We do not want children to become analytical, but we do want them to become conscious enough of story patterns that these patterns become part of their apprehensive thinking as they read. We all know the telephone book is arranged alphabetically, and use it without consciously thinking about its alphabetic structure (so, too, the Yellow Pages for business numbers). By showing children how they can imitate good patterns, we give them structures they can use as they learn to write. This enables them to practice more fully and easily in both their reading and writing. This practice maintains a wholeness of instruction, as reading and writing are taught from the same materials, eliminating any schism that may be present when reading and writing are taught as separate skills or subjects.

7

Themes

Themes may be based on almost any subject matter; from animals in general to zebras in particular; or on cars, flying, homes, trees, water, anything that interests you and your students. Themes lead to the development of concepts. Examined and reexamined by an interested group of children, themes lead to thinking, creativity, and conceptualizing, and perform as an intriguing "hook" on which to hang — quite comfortably — the teaching and learning of many new meanings and skills.

Teaching through a theme is similar to teaching through a unit; the distinction between them is mostly in the doing. A unit has a planned beginning, middle, and ending; the theme has only a beginning to stimulate exploration. However, a theme requires planning by the teacher and replanning during the investigation of the theme to reach an appropriate middle and ending. A vital factor is the acceptance of the theme by the children.

An educational theme is like a musical theme. In a musical theme the same notes recur in different rhythms, keys, forms, and cadences; the theme holds together a series of otherwise unrelated musical expressions. A fully explored theme has many variations. As a composer works with a theme he explores hundreds of variations that may never appear in the finished score. So it is with the educational theme. The exploration takes place within the classroom as the teacher and children work together. Just as a composer does not know exactly what variations will emerge and what will be the finished score, so the teacher does not know exactly what activities will effectively develop the theme nor what the culminating activity or product will be. These emerge as the theme is explored.

Just as a composer may explore for hours to produce seven minutes of music, the teacher and students may explore for days before they select the final variations of the theme to be practiced. Without trying to subtract from the importance of the skills employed in creating the variations, the crucial ingredient is the theme. Without the theme there can be no variations, no exploration of thought. The skills needed to explore an idea, to examine a theme, are acquired through the doing. *The theme is the glue that integrates otherwise unrelated, irrelevant skills and practice drills.*

Through themes children engage in an integrated learning process that allows each child to explore and respond in ways appropriate to his or her developmental needs. Themes allow sufficient time for children to learn fully and cooperatively, and to mature in thinking and understandings of concepts. Added to this, non-punitive settings foster self-esteem as each child learns and realizes that the learning is significant.

We have created a theme series of nine books, *Myself, The Sea, Fantasy, Animals, Hallowe'en, Celebrations, Fall, Winter,* and *Spring.* These combine children's observation and exploration, art, poetry, literature, non-fiction, and content teaching as children learn, record, classify, and write. The teacher initiates the teaching and then responsively selects what to do next. Skills are taught as needed and learned because they are needed as the children read, study, and record what they are learning.

The development of themes is the heart of a language program. Thoughts and the development of thoughts must be perceived by the children as the reason for language (or content area) lessons. This requires that you teach seriously and respond seriously to the children's ideas. (Note that the seriousness is in the teaching and responding, not necessarily in the ideas. We have worked delightfully, and with much laughter, with the theme of food and eating, for example.) Children sense great joy and satisfaction from working seriously and achieving.

Making skill-learning easy enough so that children focus upon meanings rather than tasks can be difficult. But it can be done. As adults, most of us write and read without consciously thinking of the process. This is our goal for children. Children will need to focus upon spelling as they learn to write, but they should never get so concerned about spelling that they forget what they are trying to say. *The skills and the learning of skills must remain subservient to thought.*

Many of the activities in this book might be described as ways of working with language so that children enjoy or have fun in learning. However, having fun while doing an exercise is not sufficient reason for doing an exercise. The exercises must emerge from serious inquiry if children are to learn how to think and to transfer their learnings to non-exercise situations. The spelling bee, for instance, is often an activity that children enjoy, but in our view it is no better at teaching spelling than writing words five times each from a weekly list. The spelling bee is likely to be fun, and the writing of words five times is likely not to be. But neither focuses upon thinking or serious thought. The focus is upon skill.

Most children become skillful when we concentrate on skill, so educators tend to conclude that there is something wrong with those children who do not respond to skill teaching. We should consider that some children cannot understand what they are supposed to be learning, and cannot make themselves learn skills for skills' sake. It is with these children particularly that the emphasis upon ideas is important. It is through the concentration upon ideas that these children come to realize what language skills they need and then willingly and knowingly practice until they learn them.

Thematic Teaching

Thematic teaching allows children to learn the skills of literacy through a content area. The skills are taught and used with a purpose, therefore they are learned with greater ease, and are usually retained to a greater degree than literacy skills taught for skills' sake. Skills learned meaningfully automatically transfer to new situations.

Thematic content falls mainly into three large areas of the curriculum:

1. social studies
2. science
3. literature

And, there are three criteria for choosing a theme:

1. the curriculum requirements
2. the children's interests
3. the materials and supplies available to the teacher

AN ELEPHANT THEME[1]

A theme we have used with great success is Elephants. The elephant theme lies mainly in the area of science, yet we dip into social studies as we study the habitat of the elephant. Literature plays a big part in our teaching as we use many chants, songs, poems, stories, and factual text to help children become literate.

We must begin any theme by filling children with the language of the theme. We begin Elephants with poetry, chants, and songs.

Elephant Poetry, Chants, and Songs

We begin by using A.A. Milne's poem *At the Zoo*.

As we read, we ask children to listen for all the animals in the poem:

At the Zoo

There are lions and roaring tigers,
    and enormous camels and things.
There are biffalo-buffalo-bisons,
    and a great big bear with wings.
There's a sort of tiny potamus,
    and a tiny nosserus too —
But I gave buns to the elephant
    when I went down to the Zoo!

---

[1] The children's examples used throughout this theme came from the classrooms of two very fine teachers.

Shirley Rainey has taught first- and second-grade children in Langley, British Columbia, Canada. The children she taught were living in a rural area of British Columbia and were from families who had lived in the area for several years.

Jackie Parker teaches first grade in Garden Grove School District in southern California. The children who wrote the examples in this theme were mainly children whose first language was not English.

There are badgers and bidgers and bodgers,
    and a Super-intendent's House,
There are masses of goats, and a Polar,
    and different kinds of mouse,
And I think there's a sort of a something
    which is called a wallaboo —
But I gave buns to the elephant
    when I went down to the Zoo!

If you try to talk to the bison,
    he never quite understands;
You can't shake hands with a mingo-
    he doesn't like shaking hands.
And lions and roaring tigers hate saying,
    "How do you do?"
But I gave buns to the elephant
    when I went down to the Zoo!

Follow-up Activities

• Ask the children to name all the animals mentioned in the poem. Record on the chalkboard all the animals children remember. Read the poem again and add to the list. Read the chalkboard list chorally.

• Have children decide what animals are real and what animals are fantasy. Have children chant the "fantasy" animals before you erase them. Children could draw the "fantasy" animals if they wish to.

• Have children decide what animals they would like to feed if they went to the zoo. List these on the chalkboard and chant the list.

• Make graphs. (1) Have children form graphs by lining up as to their favorite animal, top, page 231. (2) Then have the children make name cards and put them on the floor in place of themselves. Study this new graph on the floor. Then use blocks to build vertical columns on the floor, one block for each child's preference, bottom, page 231. (3) Finally, transfer this information to wall graphs, top, page 232, and read at varying levels of sophistication.

The photographs on pages 232–233 were taken while Mrs. Jackie Parker's grade-one children were studying animals. They created a mural around the classroom where their animals lived. The children each made a clay animal of their favorite animal living in the jungle-veldt, made habitat cubes to house their animal, and created a riddle to describe their animal, which classmates could read before opening the box to see what was inside.

- Have children build a mural by drawing their favorite animals. This mural will represent all the animals children are interested in. The study of the elephant is a small part of the larger theme, Animals.

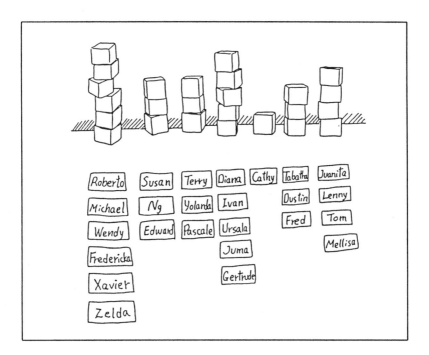

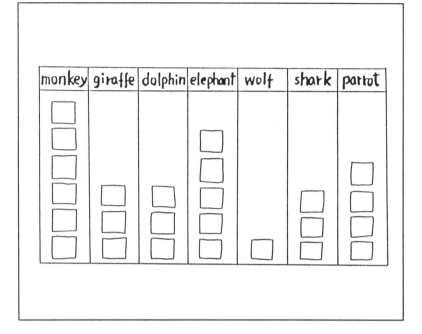

monkey	giraffe	dolphin	elephant	wolf	shark	parrot

Other Elephant Poetry

Way down south
where bananas grow
A grasshopper stepped
on an elephant's toe.
The elephant cried
with tears in his eyes
Pick on somebody
your own size.
— Anonymous

I suppose
that a nose
Is as long
as it grows.

And that's why
an elephant's
Touches
his toes!
— Anonymous

Eletelephony

Once there was an elephant
Who tried to use the telephant-
No! no! I mean an elephone
Who tried to use the telephone-
(Dear me! I am not certain quite
That even now I've got it right.)
Howe'er it was, he got his trunk
Entangled in the telephunk;
The more he tried to get it free,
The louder buzzed the telephee-
(I fear I'd better drop the song
Of elephop and telephong!)
— Laura E. Richards

Beside the Line of Elephants

I think they had no pattern
When they cut out the elephant's skin;
Some places it needs letting out,
And others, taking in.
— Edna Becker

Oliphaunt

Gray as a mouse,
Big as a house,
Nose like a snake,
I make the earth shake,
As I tramp through the grass;
Trees crack as I pass.
With horns in my mouth
I walk in the South,
Flapping big ears.
Beyond count of years
I stomp round and round,
Never lie on the ground,
Not even to die.
Oliphaunt I am,
Biggest of all,
Huge, old, and tall.
If ever you'd met me,
You wouldn't forget me.
If you never do,
You won't think I'm true;
But old Oliphaunt am I,
And I never lie.
— J.R.R. Tolkien

Holding Hands

Elephants walking
Along the trails
Are holding hands
By holding tails.

Trunks and tails
Are handy things
When elephants walk
In Circus rings.

Elephants work
And elephants play
And elephants walk
And feel so gay.

And whenever they walk-
It never fails
They're holding hands
By holding tails.
          — Lenore M. Link

The Elephant Is a Graceful Bird

The elephant is a graceful bird;
It flits from twig to twig.
It builds its nest in a rhubarb tree
And whistles like a pig.
          — Author unknown

The Elephant

When people call this beast to mind,
They marvel more and more
At such a LITTLE tail behind,
So LARGE a trunk before.
          — Hilaire Belloc

Two Kinds of Elephants

The African elephant has
huge floppy ears.
The Asian has ears
half that size.
But both have similar
trunks and tusks.
And tails and beady
black eyes.
    — Robert A. McCracken

The Handiest Nose

An elephant's nose
is the handiest nose,
the handiest nose of all-
it curves and sways
in the cleverest ways,
and trumpets a bugle call;
it reaches high
in the leafy sky
for bunches of leaves to eat,
and snuffs around
all over the ground
and dusts the elephant's feet.

An elephant's nose
is the dandiest nose,
the handiest nose of all-
for holding a palm,
when the day is calm,
as an elephant's parasol,
and making a spray
for a sultry day,
and a hose for sprinkling too,
and a hand to wag
near a peanut bag
when you watch him at the zoo.

Oh, an elephant's nose
is fun to see,
an elephant's nose is fine;
it's clever as ever
a nose can be
but I'm glad it isn't mine.
        — Aileen Fisher

Enormous

The elephant is large in size
With two huge ears
And two big eyes.
It has a trunk, a sort of nose,
That hangs in front
Down to its toes.
It snatches food
It pulls down trees.
Be careful when
It has to sneeze.
        — Robert A. McCracken

The Elephant

Elephants stand huge and grey.
They sleep or lumber through the day.
At night they feed on shoots and leaves.
They roll in mud. They uproot trees.
They like to run. They like to play
To wade in water there to spray.
With their huge feet they sometimes stomp
On shrubs and bushes as they romp.
Elephants do whatever they please.
Be well prepared in case they sneeze.
        — Robert A. McCracken

Memory

They say that an elephant
Will never forget you.
But how can he remember
If he's never met you?
    — Robert A. McCracken

A Nose

The elephant has a long, long trunk
Which really is his great big nose.
How would you feel if you had one
To scratch your itchy toes?
    — Robert A. McCracken

An Elephant Family

If you should ever happen to meet
An elephant herd upon the street,
Father's the bull,
Mother's the cow,
And baby's the calf.
The mother and father
Would trumpet at you,
But the baby might make you laugh!
    — Robert A. McCracken

An Elephant Countdown

Children learn the poem initially without the number equations. The computation can be taught later, and children can then chant in two parts.

Ten fat elephants frolicking in a line   10
One ran away: that left nine. $\underline{-1}$
       9

Nine fat elephants frolicking through the gate   9
One ran away: that left eight. $\underline{-1}$
       8

Eight fat elephants frolicking at 7-Eleven   8
One ran away: that left seven.   -1
                                                  7

Seven fat elephants frolicking on the bricks   7
One ran away: that left six.   -1
                                                  6

Six fat elephants frolicking on the drive   6
One ran away: that left five.   -1
                                                  5

Five fat elephants frolicking on the floor   5
One ran away: that left four.   -1
                                                  4

Four fat elephants frolicking by the tree   4
One ran away: that left three.   -1
                                                  3

Three fat elephants frolicking at the zoo   3
One ran away: that left two.   -1
                                                  2

Two fat elephants frolicking in the sun   2
One ran away: that left one.   -1
                                                  1

One fat elephant frolicking for fun   1
One ran away: that left none.   -1
                                                  0

   — Robert A. McCracken

Elephant Chants and Fingerplays

Elephant

Right foot, left foot, see me go.
I am gray and big and slow.
I come walking down the street
With my trunk and four big feet.
— Anonymous

Five Little Elephants

Five little elephants
Rowing toward the shore.
One fell in.
Then there were four.

Four little elephants
Climbing up a tree.
One slid down.
Then there were three.

Three little elephants
Living in the zoo.
One walked off.
Then there were two.

Two little elephants
Playing in the sun.
One fell asleep.
Then there was one.

One little elephant
Isn't any fun.
Abra-ca-da-bra!
Then there were none!
-Author unknown

Ten Little Elephants

One little, two little,
Three little elephants.
Four little, five little,
Six little elephants.
Seven little, eight little,
Nine little elephants,
Ten little elephant calves.

The Elephant Carries a Great Big Trunk

The elephant carries a great big trunk;
He never packs it with clothes;
It has no lock. It has no key,
But it goes wherever he goes.
    — Anonymous

Oliver the Elephant (from "Move Over Mother Goose")
(An Action Verse)

(Sneeze) Oliver Elephant happened to sneeze,
(Fall to knees) And all of a sudden he fell to his knees!
(Struggle) It's hard to get up
(Wipe brow) When you're built like a truck
(Get up easily) But Oliver did it with ease.
    — Ruth I. Dowell

Penelope Elephant
(An Action Verse)

Penelope Elephant's yellow umbrella
(Look up) Got stuck in the top of a tree.
(Sit down) This elegant elephant lady decided
(Settle down) To have a cup of tea:
(Drink "tea") "I'll sip my drink and sit a while,
And soon the wind will blow;
(Look up & And down will come my yellow umbrella
follow umbrella) And off again I'll go."
    — Ruth I. Dowell

The Elephant Rhyme

The elephant goes like this and that
He's terribly big
And he's terribly fat.
He has no fingers,
He has no toes,
But goodness, gracious, what a nose!
— Traditional

Elephant Songs

a) One Elephant Went Out to Play
This traditional song (see pages 244–245) is part of a
song teaching package from McCracken Educational
Services.
b) The Cow and the Elephant, by Claude Clayton Smith

General Directions for Teaching Poetry

Teach Informally
Every day, read a favorite elephant poem or chant. Reread
the poems children particularly like many times. Children
need to hear the sound of fine language often. They join in
as soon as they can on the repeated parts.

Teach Formally
Work with a poem or chant for a week. Allow children to
enjoy it as they chant along, bounce the rhythms, and
sense the meanings. Place the text in the pocket chart
phrase by phrase or line by line and work with it in various ways:

• Track the words in the pocket chart as you read or chant.
  When the children know the poem or chant, have them take
  turns tracking the words as the class chants.

ONE
ELEPHANT
WENT OUT
TO PLAY

Traditional Song

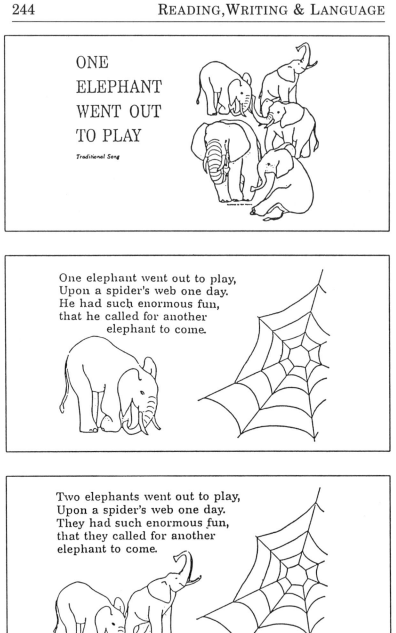

One elephant went out to play,
Upon a spider's web one day.
He had such enormous fun,
that he called for another
elephant to come.

Two elephants went out to play,
Upon a spider's web one day.
They had such enormous fun,
that they called for another
elephant to come.

Three elephants went out to play,
Upon a spider's web one day.
They had such enormous fun,
that they called for another
elephant to come.

Four elephants went out to play,
Upon a spider's web one day.
They had such enormous fun,
that they called for another
elephant to come.

Five elephants went out to play,
Upon a spider's web one day.
They had such enormous fun,
but there were no more
elephants left to come.

• When a poem, chant, or song is memorized, use that memorized language to help children learn about print. Distribute the word or phrase cards to the children and have them re-build the text in the pocket chart. Guide the children through this activity one or two times. Then place the word or phrase cards in the language center so that children can work independently with them.

Known poems are printed on word cards, one word per card. These word cards are jumbled and placed in a large envelope. Have the children work together in small groups to sequence the text. Include separate cards for punctuation if you wish children to practice that.

Memorizing Poetry

Memorizing a poem often involves four steps:

1. Put the poem in the pocket chart on phrase cards.

2. Have the children echo the poem phrase by phrase as you chant it with them.

3. Distribute the phrase cards among the children, who place them in the pocket chart in correct sequence. Help if necessary.

4. With the text in the pocket chart, tell the children to close their eyes. Turn over one card and ask, "What did I turn over?" When they open their eyes, have the children identify the word or phrase. Leaving the card turned over, repeat the process until most or all of the cards are turned over. Then have the children chant the whole poem with you tracking, pointing to each blank card. (With young children, this might take several days.)

Teaching Poetry Through Drama

Some poems lend themselves to dramatization.

Use drama to develop the meaning and feel for a poem. Work with the whole class. Everyone does all the parts, initially, at least. As teacher, you may need to "ham" the poem until children get used to the fun of acting. Much drama can be done with one hand and the forearm of the other arm.

General Learning Practices
• Hang the poem text in the room where children can see it. Many will read it and chant it to themselves during "blah" times of the day.

• Assign three or four children to print the text on a large poster and to illustrate the text.

• Have the class create Big Books. Each child can illustrate one phrase or two or three lines and print the lyric under the illustration. The book is then bound for class use. Children may choose to make individual books of their favorite poems.

• Have children keep a poetry journal in which they write their favorite poems. They may illustrate their journals.

• Put stanzas of unknown poems on phrase cards and assign groups of four or five children to construct the poem.

Children Write Their Own Poetry
a) Read Dennis Lee's *Willoughby, Wallaby, Woo* to the children, then place the phrases in the pocket chart. Track the words as children sing or chant.

Willoughby wallaby wee,
An elephant sat on me.
Willaby wallaby woo,
An elephant sat on you.

Willaby wallaby wustin,
An elephant sat on Justin.
Willaby wallaby wania,
An elephant sat on Tania.

Next, make a set of cards that contains each child's name. Have the children decide on a rhyming word for each name. Place the new cards in the pocket chart, two verses at a time, and have the children sing along. For example:

Willaby wallaby bendy
An elephant sat on Wendy.

Willaby wallaby matherine
An elephant sat on Catherine.

Mix the cards and pull out a few every day to sing. It's always a surprise to see whose names will turn up. With the cards made it is easy to next make a class song book.

Children will also enjoy writing two or three verses in their personal language books, using their friends' or relatives' names. The two examples (shown opposite) are from Shirley Rainey's class in Langley, British Columbia.

b) Use the poem *Rules* by Karla Kuskin. Shown on pages 250–251 is the McCracken Educational Services poster of *Rules*. Read and enjoy the poem. Then, make up fun rules for elephants. For example:

Where shouldn't elephants go?
What shouldn't elephants wear?
What shouldn't elephants use?
What shouldn't elephants sing?
What shouldn't elephants eat?
What shouldn't elephants dance?

Willaby wollaby wooper
An elephant sat on Hooper!

Julie
Grade 1

(Hooper is Julie's dog!)

Willoby wolla by wamma
An elephant sat on grama.

Joey
Grade I

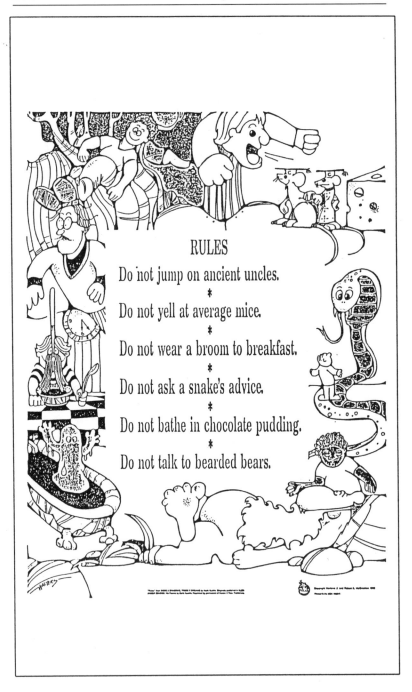

Do not smoke cigars on sofas.

Do not dance on velvet chairs.

Do not take a whale to visit
Russell's mother's cousin's yacht.

And whatever else you do do
It is better you
Do not.

Karla Kuskin

Never let an elephant ride on
your bike.

Jennifer   Grade 2

The example shown above is from Shirley Rainey's grade-two class and shows Jennifer's picture and writing.

c) Write an elephant counting poem. For example this countdown by Bob McCracken.

One elephant feeling fine.
Two elephants out to dine.
Three elephants eating hay.
Four elephants out to play.
Five elephants walking by.
Six elephants reaching high.

Brainstorm what elephants do. Their ideas can be fact or fiction. For example, elephants:

go to the grocery store
ride in a Volkswagen
wear designer blue jeans
eat spaghetti with a spoon
ride rocket ship to the moon
read *Charlotte's Web*
play baseball after school
ski downhill in a race.

Make certain you get forty to fifty ideas on the chalkboard. Children read the ideas in chorus, and then choose their favorites to include in their countdowns. First and second graders should not worry about rhyme. If some children can rhyme their countdown, that's fine, but most children will find it too difficult.

d) Use *I Like Bugs* by Margaret Wise Brown. Our poster form is shown on the next page.

Work with this poem in the pocket chart. Chant it, and snap, clap, to the rhythm. Feel the rhyme, accenting it as you chant. When children know the poem, substitute the word "elephants" for the word "bugs." Put the word "elephants" on as many cards as you need and cover up the word "bugs" with the "elephant" cards in the pocket chart. Read the new poem.

Now to create an entirely new poem, have the children think of other describing words and other prepositional phrases. Chant several aloud before you have children write their own. Read and enjoy Jason's, top left on page 256 (from Shirley Rainey's grade-two class).

A modification of this poem for first-grade children allows them to write with ease. Shirley Rainey wrote this example pattern for her first-grade children:

I LIKE BUGS
Margaret Wise Brown

I like bugs.
Black bugs,
Green bugs,

Bad bugs,
Mean bugs,
Any kind of bug,
I like bugs.

A bug on the sidewalk,
A bug in the grass,
A bug in the rug,
A bug in a glass,
I like bugs.

Round bugs,
Shiny bugs,
Fat bugs,

Buggy bugs,
Big bugs,
Lady bugs,
I like bugs.

I like elephants
All kinds of elephants.
_____ elephants
_____ elephants
and _____ elephants
_____ elephants
I like elephants!

First-grade children brainstormed many adjectives for elephants, then they wrote the pattern with ease. For example, Brent, in Shirley Rainey's first-grade classroom, got quite carried away with his use of adjectives! (right page 256)

It is important that children be encouraged and allowed to make many variations on a pattern.

e) Use prepositional phrases within a pattern.

Brainstorm places where the children might see an elephant. Record their responses on the chalkboard. For example:

at the zoo
in the jungle

Get at least thirty to forty phrases on the chalkboard. Have the children chorally chant the phrases.

Create the following pattern in the pocket chart.

Elephants
Elephants _____,
Elephants _____,*
Elephants _____,
Elephants _____,*
Elephants! Elephants! Elephants!
Elephants everywhere!

Big elephants
Saggy elephants
Tame elephants
Baggy elephants
Any kind of elephants
I like elephants!
An elephant in a zoo
An elephant in a park
An elephant at a game farm
An elephant in the dark.
I like elephants!
Baby elephants
Fat elephants
Lasy elephants
Silly elephants
fast elephants
Slow elephants
I like elephants!

By Jason

I like elephants
All kinds of elephants
chubby strong elephants
fast lost elephants
sloppy baggy elephants
loud mad elephants
old hairy elephants
giant fat elephants
quiet trained elephants
cute wild elephants
They are the kinds I like
the most. by Brent Brooks

Elephants in the jungle,
Elephants in a river,
Elephants in the circus,
Elephants in a shiver,
ELEPHANTS! ELEPHANTS! ELEPHAN-
TS!
Elephants in a hole,
Elephants on the run,
Elephants in the rain,
Elephants in the sun
ELEPHANTS! ELEPHANTS! ELEPHANTS!
Elephants everywhere!

by David Brooks

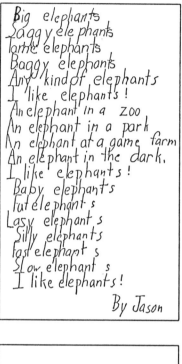

Have the children practice saying the brainstormed phrases aloud in the blank spaces of the pattern. Second-third- and fourth-grade children may try to rhyme the lines that are marked with asterisks.

David, from Shirley Rainey's second-grade class, wrote the poem shown at lower left opposite page.

Read to the Children About Elephants

There is a wealth of children's fiction about elephants. The following is a representative selection that you can read to the children. (All the books are also listed in the Bibliography of Books for Children, page 285.)

Children's Fiction Books About Elephants

Ah-Choo by Mercer Mayer.
Alexander's Midnight Snack: A Little Elephant's ABC by Catherine Stock.
Babar's Picnic by Laurent de Brunhoff.
A Beast Called an Elephant by Philip Stong.
The Biggest Nose by Kathy Caple.
The Bird Who Was an Elephant by Aleph Kamal.
Boris Bad Enough by Robert Kraus.
But No Elephants by Jerry Smath.
Cat on the Mat by Brian Wildsmith.
The Day It Rained Elephants by Martin Waddell.
The Elephant by Colin and Jacqui Hawkins.
Elephant Cat by Nicola Bayley.
Elephant Cat by Chris Riddell.
The Elephant in Duck's Garden by Judy Delton.
Elephant and Mouse Celebrate Halloween by Lois Grambling.
The Elephant and the Bad Baby by Elfrida Vipont.
The Elephant and the Scrubforest by David J. Taylor.
The Elephant in the Dark by Carol Carrick.
The Elephant's Child by Rudyard Kipling from the Just So Stories.

Ella by Bill Peet.
Emily's Own Elephant by Philipps Pearce.
Encore for Elephant by Bill Peet.
Esther's Trunk: An Elephantasy by Jez Alborough.
Faithful Elephants: A True Story of Animals, People and War by Yukio Tsuchiya.
Jamba the Elephant by Theodore Waldeck.
Little Wild Elephant by Anna Michel.
Mogul and Me by Peter Cuming.
Mouse and Elephant by Matthias Hoppe.
Nathan and Nicholas Alexander by Lulu Delacre.
Nathan's Balloon Adventure by Lulu Delacre.
Ollie the Elephant by Burny Bos (a picture book).
One Little Elephant by Colin West.
Peel — The Extraordinary Elephant by Susan Joyce.
The Right Number of Elephants by Jill Sheppard.
Rosie, The Dancing Elephant by Maureen Daly.
The Story of a Patchwork Elephant by David Elmer McKee.
Ten Little Elephants by Robert Leydenfrost.
Time for School, Nathan by Lulu Delacre.
The Travels of Babar by Jean de Brunhoff.
The Trouble With Elephants by Chris Riddell.
The Trunk by Brian Wildsmith.
The Twenty-Elephant Restaurant by Russell Hoban.
Uncle Elephant by Arnold Lobel.
The Way Home by Judith Benet Richardson.
We'll Ride Elephants Through Brooklyn by Susan L. Roth.
When the Elephant Walks by Keiko Kaza.
Where Can an Elephant Hide? by David McPhail.

Children Write Fantasy

When the children have heard many fantasies about elephants, they may enjoy writing their own fantasy.

Place the following story frame on the chalkboard or on butcher paper.

Once there was an/a _____ elephant who had always wished to _____. One day an/a came and granted the wish.

_____

_____ .

On Monday, spend five or ten minutes discussing possible ways to complete the frame. On Tuesday, Wednesday, and Thursday, do the same. Ten minutes spent on four consecutive days does much more to produce creative ideas than does one forty-minute oral session. On Friday, ask the children to write their own fantasy. See next page for examples of first-grade writing.

Shirley Rainey's second-grade students used the frame as a jumping off point. Once they began their stories, the frame was ignored. Jill's story is a good example of this.

Once there was a wrinkly African elephant who wished he could be in a parade. One day a beautiful fairy came and granted his wish. After the fairy left the elephant went shopping and bought a fancy blanket to put on his back when he was in the parade. But after a little while the elephant sat down. He was tired of walking. Then he fell asleep in the middle of the parade. He slept and slept. Then he awoke. He got up and started to walk again. When the parade was over the elephant went on some rides But all the rides he went on he broke them all. The elephant was sad. He did not want to be in a parade again and he didn't.

On page 261 are two fantasies from Jackie Parker's first-grade classroom. Jackie teaches mainly E.S.L. children in Garden Grove, California. This work was done in the last month of first grade, as Jackie was teaching an Animal Theme.

January 31

Once there was a little elephant who had always wished to fly. Then one day an elf came and granted his wish. So he was happy.
He flew to White Rock. He had some fish and chips and he went to the beach.
He was very happy.

by Chris
Grade 1

January 31

Once there was a sad elephant who had always wished to fly. Then one day a fairy prinsis came and granted his wish So he could fly. he was so happy that he danst. he floo to canada.

by Janet
Grade 1

January 31

Once there was a cute elephant who had always wished to have a ferrari. Then one day a green leprechaun came and granted his wish. So Then he got into his ferrari and went to his friends and he asked them if they wanted a ride. And they said yes. So then he gave them a ride. The elephants thought it was scary because it went so fast.

by Darren
Grade 1

These stories are the fantasies of three children from Shirley Rainey's first-grade group. These children came to school with a good language base, and a fine experience in kindergarten. This work was done mid-year (January) in the first grade.

Once upon a time there was a elephant. His name Saggy Baggy Elephant. He live in the Jungle. He is fat. He have two sharep tust. He have a long nose. He have little eyes and he can't see very well. Saggy Baggy meet His friend every day. Quan

Once upon a time There was a Elephant His name was Johnathen He had two floppy ears I like him. Suddenly a Fox came and ate him and that Was The end of The Elephant.

Anthiny

Building a Word Bank with Children

Building an Elephant word bank will increase the children's vocabulary. Have them use this vocabulary in writing structures so that it becomes internalized.

1. Work at the chalkboard initially. You will need a large space to record three or four columns of words.

2. You need two copies of the word bank. If the children are able to print quickly and legibly, choose two of them to act as secretaries. (If your children are not yet able to print legibly, "borrow" two fourth- or fifth-grade children to act as your secretaries.) Give each secretary a felt pen and word cards and ask them to record each word as you print words on the chalkboard. This will give you two sets of word cards. One of these sets goes on the wall for reference as children write, and the other set is used for hands-on manipulation of language.

3. Place the word *elephants* on the chalkboard. Ask children to tell you what kinds of elephants they know about. Record their answers on the chalkboard, and have children chant the list each time a new word is recorded.

grey elephants
baby
huge
enormous
mother
wrinkly
father
bull
saggy
big
old
mad
cute
fat
sad
hungry

4. Record all the words the children give you. When you have recorded twenty words or more for first grade and thirty to forty adjectives for older children, work with those words in the pocket chart. Collect one set of printed words from the secretaries and place them randomly in the pocket chart, doubling the adjectives. For example:

> father   old   elephants
> huge   hungry
> baby   cute

As children chant the list, track to see if the words "sound" correct, and if they make "sense." Ask the children, "Should we say, `father old elephants' or `old father elephants'?" and so on. Correct the words in the pocket chart and leave them there (left, below).

5. Continue to build the word bank on the chalkboard. Ask children to tell you what elephants do. Record the words on the chalkboard as before and have the children chant the entire list of verbs as each new word is added. The adjusted pocket chart is shown at right, below.

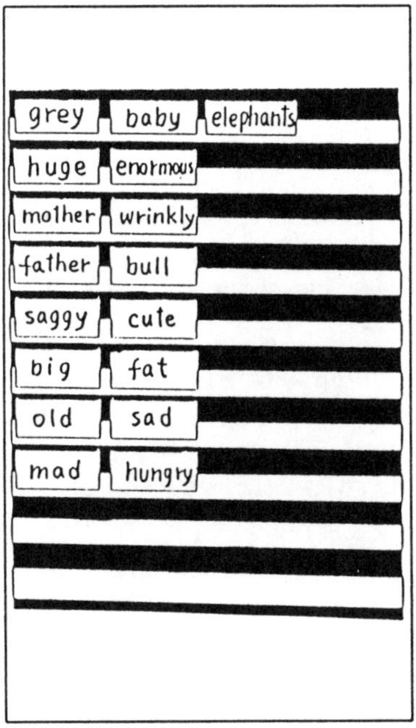

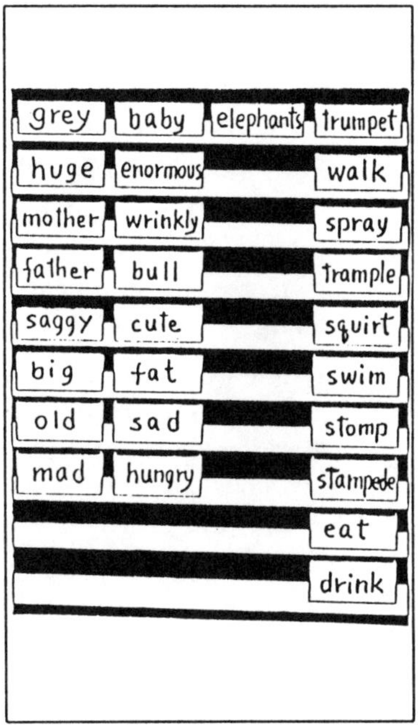

January 24

Wrinkly African elephants work. Humungus elephants spray water. Lucky gray elephants run all over. Nice mother elephants play with there babies. Hot muddy elephants swim.

by Kelly   Grade I

6. Now track the words to build sentences for children. Have the children chant as you track.

huge grey elephants trumpet
fat mother elephants eat
cute baby elephants run (and so on)

7. After you have modeled many sentences, let the children take their turns. They can use the pointer and track their own created sentences while the rest of the class chants along.

8. When much oral work has been done, this lesson is completed by having the children write sentences in their language books. Some children will write six to eight sentences, while others will do two or three sentences.

Kelly, in Shirley Rainey's first-grade class, wrote the sentences shown above.

9. The next day, continue building the word bank by adding prepositional phrases. Ask the children where they might see an elephant and record the phrases as before,

having the children chant with each new addition.

in the jungle
by the river
under trees
in the water
in the mud
near the pond
with their babies
in Africa
in the dirt
in the dust
by the grassland
all over India
in a herd
in the shade
under the blue skies
near the zebras

10. Practice these phrases by using them in song. They can be
    sung easily to the tune of *The Farmer in the Dell.* You
    might sing:

Elephants in the mud,
Elephants in the mud,
Rolling, rolling, rolling, rolling,
Elephants in the mud.
or
Elephants under trees,
Elephants under trees,
Eating, eating, eating, eating,
Elephants under trees.
or
Elephants in the water,
Elephants in the water,
Swimming, squirting, rolling, spraying,
Elephants in the water.

You should model many times before you ask the children
to make up their own songs. Children love to sing songs
they have made up. If children are too shy to sing by
themselves, ask others to sing with them.

This oral work can be followed by building a class song book with each child contributing a page of written verse with illustrations.

11. Your chalkboard will now look like this:

grey	elephants	trumpet	in the jungle
baby		walk	by the river
huge		spray	under trees
enormous		trample	in the water
mother		squirt	in the mud
wrinkly		swim	near the pond
father		stomp	with their babies
bull		stampede	in Africa
saggy		eat	in the dirt
big		drink	in the dust
old		thump	by the grassland
mad		roll	all over India
cute		run	in a herd
fat		sleep	in the shade
sad		pull	under the blue skies
hungry		push	near the zebras

Use these words to develop sentence sense. Model by tracking the words and creating sentences that "sound right" and that "make good sense." For example, track:

Enormous mother elephants walk with their babies.
Huge bull elephants stampede in Africa.
Cute baby elephants sleep in the shade.
Wrinkly grey elephants swim in the water.
Big old elephants stomp in a herd.

Have the children use the manipulative set of cards to create a variety of sentences.

1. Put the children into groups of four, making sure the children in each group are of mixed skill ability. Give each group:

- four adjectives
- two "elephant" cards
- four verbs
- four prepositional phrases

2. Ask the children to build two sentences with the cards. The children move the cards around to build sentences similar to the type they have practiced orally. (See next page) As each group completes its two sentences, have them read their sentences aloud to the class. For example:

Hungry fat elephants eat under the blue skies.
Enormous grey elephants run in the jungle.

3. When a group has made several sentences, we challenge them to transform the sentence, writing a sentence in more than one way. For example, the group has created the following sentence:

Hungry fat elephants eat under the blue skies.

We say, "Can you use the same cards in a different order and still make good sense?"
We help as necessary to get the children to create other sensible sentences:

Fat hungry elephants eat under the blue skies.
Under the blue skies fat hungry elephants eat.
Under the blue skies hungry fat elephants eat.

4. Collect the cards when children have had twenty to thirty minutes of manipulating cards. To do this, ask each child to pick up two cards and to share the remaining cards with the group. Then, collect the cards in the following manner:

- Ask the children to hold up the cards that describe elephants. Collect these and place them together on the chalkboard ledge.

- Ask the children to hold up the cards that tell what elephants do. Collect these and place them in another group on the chalkboard ledge.

- Ask the children to hold up the cards that tell where they might see an elephant. Collect, and place in another group.

- Ask the children to hold up the cards that say, "elephants." Collect and place in another group.

5. If applicable to your grade level, have the children place correct captions on the top of each group of words:

nouns
verbs
adjectives
prepositional phrases

6. For older children, challenge them in the following ways:

- Give the children more word cards to work with (for example, eight or ten adjectives, eight or ten verbs and prepositional phrases). This allows for many more transformations.

- Brainstorm adverbial phrases. Place these on word cards and use them when building sentences. Ask the children when the elephants do things. For example: "When do elephants go to the watering hole?"

after the sun sets
by the light of the moon
under the noon sun
as the stars twinkled
by dawn's early light
as the sun rose
when the first pink rays appeared
in the heat of the day

Have the children experiment with these new phrases to see how many ways they can fit them into the basic sentence patterns.

Write Lists and Contrasts
Using Specific Parts of the Word Bank

• Brainstorm things that elephants can't do. Have fun with
this. You might need to model some fun answers for
children. Write their responses on the chalkboard. Chant
each response as it has been recorded, then chant the whole
column when finished. Try to get twenty to thirty responses
in first grade and more with older children. A sample
chalkboard might look like this:

> Elephants can't...
> wear long underwear.
> lick a chocolate ice cream cone.
> go on a bus.
> ride a unicycle.
> go to town on a skateboard.
> float down in a parachute.
> go to a movie.

Now work orally with children using the frame in the pocket chart.

Elephants can _____.
Elephants can _____.
Elephants can _____.
But elephants can't _____.

Have the children use the verb column from the word bank and the brainstormed list from the chalkboard to complete the contrast. When much oral work has been done, children may write contrasts in their language books. For example:

Elephants can stampede.
Elephants can trample.
Elephants can sleep.
But elephants can't wear lipstick and nail polish.

• Ask the children what kinds of elephants they wouldn't like to meet at the zoo. Record their answers on the chalkboard, chanting as before. For example:

mad
ugly
hungry
monster
stampeding
bull
angry
frightened
wild

Work orally with this chalkboard list and the adjectives in the word bank to complete the following frame.

I like _____ elephants.
I like _____ elephants.
I like _____ elephants.
But I don't like _____ elephants.

When much oral work has been done, children may write these contrasts in their language books. For example:

> I like enormous mother elephants.
> I like cute baby elephants.
> I like old grey elephants.
> But I don't like ugly bull elephants.

• Ask the children where they would not see an elephant. List their answers on the chalkboard, chanting them as they are being recorded. For example:

> in an ice-cream parlor
> on an airplane
> on the escalator
> in an elevator
> under the covers on my bed
> in the Safeway
> by my desk

Now have the children practice the following frame orally, combining the prepositional phrases recorded on the chalkboard with those in the word bank. For example:

> You could see an elephant _____.
> You could see an elephant _____.
> You could see an elephant _____.
> But you couldn't see an elephant _____.

In their langauge books, the children might write:

> You could see an elephant in the mud.
> You could see an elephant in the shade.
> You could see an elephant under trees.
> But you couldn't see an elephant on the escalator.

Factual Books About Elephants

All books are listed in the Bibliography of Books for Children, page 285.

A Closer Look at Elephants by John Holbrook.
A Year in the Life by John Stidworthy and Rosalind Hewitt.
America's First Elephant by Robert McClung.
Elephant by Byron Barton.
Elephant by Mary Hoffman.
Elephants by Edmund Rogers.
Elephants by Elsa Z. Posell.
Elephants by Miriam Schlein (in Jane Goodall's *Animal World*).
Elephants by Cynthia Overbeck.
Elephants by J. Ele.
Elephants by John B. Wexo.
Elephants by Michael Bright.
Elephants by Joe van Wormer.
Elephants by Norman S. Barrett.
Elephants by Reinhard Kelsey.
Elephants by Barbara Taylor Cork.
Elephant Baby by Udiavar G. Rao.
Elephant Bathes by Derek Hall.
Elephant Crossing by Toshi Yoshida.
Elephant Facts by Bob Barner.
Elephant Kingdom by Henry Neil Marshall.
Elephants and Mammoths by Gwynne Vevers.
Elephants in the Wild by Cliff Moon.
Elephants Live Here by Irmengarde Eberle.
Elephants, the Last of the Land Giants by Anthony Ravielle.
Elephants, the Vanishing Giants by Dan Freeman.
From Trunk to Tail: Elephants Legendary and Real by Suzanne Jurmain.
Jumbo, the Biggest Elephant in the World by Florence M. Burns.
Little Wild Elephant by Anna Michel.
Speak to the Earth by Vivienne de Watterville.
Suleiman the Elephant by Margret Rettich.

Tail Toes Eyes Ears Nose by Marilee Burton.
Ten Things I Know About Elephants by Wendy Wax.
The Elephant Book by Dennis Pepper.
The Love of Elephants by Neil Murray.
The Trumpeting Herd by Guy Muldoon.
Wonders of Elephants by Sigmund A. Lavine.

WORKING WITH E.S.L. CHILDREN

Jackie Parker read many factual elephant books to her first-grade E.S.L. children. She then asked them to tell her everything they knew about elephants. Jackie recorded this information in simple sentence form on the chalkboard. The children read the sentences aloud three or four times before they were asked to choose their favorites and write them in their language books.

Four examples from these lessons are on pages 275 and 276.

Children Like to Write Silly Sentences

Tell the children to make up silly sentences that will make you laugh. Here's an example from Shirley Rainey's first-grade classroom.

Funny silly elephants do tricks on a cake.

Beginning Paragraph Writing

Read factual stories about elephants to the children. (You might read about baby elephants first.) Then ask the children what they have learned and record their answers on the chalkboard. Ask questions such as:

What is a baby elephant called?
Where does a baby elephant live?
How big is it at birth?

Elephants
Elephants are big and strong
Elephants eat fruit and grass.
Elephants have good memories.
Elephants eat a lot.
Elephants pull up trees
by the trunk and the
roots Elephants have 2 tusks
Elephants drink a lot of water
Hue

Elephants
Elephants are big and fat
Elephants are big
Elephants are wrinkly
Elephants have good memriy
Elephants like to eat grass and
frot Elephants live to be old
Elephants use ther trunk for a
hand Elephants are sliong
Elephants live in herds
Elephants tusks are sharp
and pointy Elephants have a
long long trunk Elephants
arre smart Elephants
have 2 tusks. Henry

Elephants
are big and strong. Elephants
have strong, big feet. Elephants
eat grass. Elephants are gray
and big. Elephants drink water.
and blow it out.
Elephants have 2 tusks.
Elephants have big toenails.
Elephant babies   are about
our size.
Elephants have two big ears.
Elephants can squash things
Elephants like to take baths.
Elephants have long tusks:
They are about ten   feet

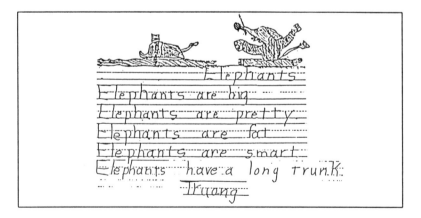

long when they are old.
Elephants have a long long
trunk
Elephants live in herds.
Duy

Elephants
Elephants are big
Elephants are pretty
Elephants are fat
Elephants are smart
Elephants have a long trunk.
Kuang

What does it look like?
What does it eat?
How long is it a baby, staying with its mother?
How big will it get?

As you ask these questions, record children's answers on the chalkboard in factual story form. For example:

Baby Elephants
A baby elephant is called a calf. It stays close to its mother, in the family group. A new baby stands about three feet tall and is often covered with reddish-brown hair. It drinks the milk its mother makes in her body. Calves stay with their families. Families stay together except for the young males who leave the family at about fourteen years old. Elephants never stop growing. The oldest bull elephants grow to about twelve feet tall, and weigh seven tons.

(This is a long story. Beginning stories should use only three or four questions.)

When you have finished writing the factual story on the chalkboard, have children read it back immediately as you track. Then read the story again with children just before they go home in the afternoon. If you wish, the story can be typed, duplicated, and given to children to paste in their language books for their own information and for individual reading practice. First- and second-grade children need much modeling before they are required to write factual stories or paragraphs independently.

You might try writing class paragraphs from questions on the following topics:

- the elephant family
- bull elephants
- what elephants can do
- playtime for calves
- how the elephant moves
- elephant communication
- what elephants eat
- remarkable facts about elephants

Sophisticating Paragraph Writing

Read factual information about elephants to children, asking them to listen particularly for *what elephants have.* When you have completed the oral reading, record the children's answers in simple sentence form on sentence strips. For example:

> Elephants have long trunks.
> Elephants have wrinkly skin.
> Elephants have big toe nails.
> Elephants have big tusks.
> Elephants have big ears.
> Elephants have round legs.
> Elephants have little eyes.
> Elephants have little tails.
> Elephants have huge bodies.
> Elephants are grey.

Ask the children to read these sentences aloud as you place them in the pocket chart. Ask them, "Do they sound interesting? If you were going to write a letter to your grandma telling her what you have learned about elephants, would you write like this? What would be the best sentence to start with?"

When we did this with children, one child said, "We should begin with 'elephants have huge bodies.'" We took the sentence from the pocket chart and asked if there was another sentence we could put with this one. Another child answered, "Elephants are grey." We took that sentence out of the pocket chart and asked how we could put these two sentences together to make one sentence. A child answered, "Elephants have huge, grey bodies." We wrote on the chalkboard, "Elephants have huge, grey bodies with."

We then asked what we could use to complete the sentence. A child answered, "wrinkly skin."

Now our first sentence read:

Elephants have huge, grey bodies with wrinkly skin.

We then decided to combine all the sentences that had to do with the elephant's head. We used a "commas-in-a-series" structure to record this and added it to our first sentence:

Elephants have huge, grey bodies with wrinkly skin. They have big ears, little eyes, tusks, and long trunks.

The remainder of the sentences were combined, so that our chalkboard story looked like this:

Elephants have huge, grey bodies with wrinkly skin. They have big ears, little eyes, tusks, and long trunks. They have large, round legs with big toe nails, but they have tiny tails.

This is not a wonderful paragraph, but we were beginning to teach children how to organize facts and how to combine them to form complex sentences. After five or six lessons of this type, a second-grade child in Shirley Rainey's classroom wrote the two paragraphs shown on page 280.

At the conclusion of this section, children should understand the following:

- Elephants are mammals.
- Elephants are the largest animals living on land.
- Elephant's natural habitats are Africa and Asia.
- Elephants need lots of space to live in because they need to eat so much. Spaces that are large enough for elephants are quickly disappearing. Elephants are becoming an endangered species.
- Elephants are vegetarians. They do not hunt other animals for meat to eat. They live quite peaceful, family-type lives. They are often called "the friendly giants."

January 25

Elephants have trunks, they use them for many things. Elephants put mud, sand and dust on there back to cool themselves. There trunk is really their top lip and nose. Elephants pick up logs with their trunks. They have two things at the end of there nose like fingers. Elephants trunks are used for feeling things. The important thing about their trunks are that they can smell things and they eat with their trunk. They make sounds with there trunks.

January 26

Elephants are vegetarians. When they are in the wild they eat plants, berries, leaves and grass. Sometimes elephants eat bark. When elephants are in the zoo they eat carrots, cabbage, peanuts, hay and patatoes. Elephants drink 30 gallons of water a day. They eat all day because they have huge bodies.

You can also teach the children these interesting facts about elephants.

- Elephants live in very warm countries, so they have developed a way to keep cool. They adjust their cooling systems by flapping their huge ears quickly or slowly. They also cool themselves by burping up water from their stomachs and hosing it over their ears and shoulders with their trunks.

- Elephants are one of the few animals able to use "tools." They often use termite hills like we use sandpaper, scrubbing away at the itchy parts of their bodies. An elephant will also hold a stick in its trunk and use it for scratching between the legs. Elephants often rip out bundles of grass with their trunks to use to clean their ear openings.

- The trunk of an elephant is a combination of nose and upper lip. It is as versatile as a human arm, able to pick up a single blade of grass. The tip of the trunk is really the tip of the nose with two nostrils showing. Baby elephants take a long time learning how to use their trunks. They bring their mouths down to the water level until they learn to use their trunks as drinking hoses.

- Elephant mothers are kind and gentle to their calves. Calves are bluish-black, covered with reddish fuzzy hair. They drink ten quarts of their mother's milk every day. Elephant babies love close body contact. Their mothers use their trunks to soothe them and to guide their footing. Mothers will stand still in the heat of the midday sun to provide shade for their sleeping babies.

- Elephants can travel twenty miles a day, and will march for miles to reach water holes or salt licks. They trot (they cannot gallop) very quickly, outrunning humans on a short run, but they heat up quickly, and must slow their pace for longer runs.

- Elephants love a mud bath. The thick mud cools their skins and protects them from insects and heat. The bath is a part of their daily hygiene.

- An elephant's tusks grow throughout its life. They are used for daily chores. Elephants use their tusks as levers when pulling up bundles of grass. The largest tusk on record weighed two hundred and twenty-five pounds (102 kg) and was twenty-six feet (8 m) long. Many elephants are killed because of the value of their ivory tusks. Two-thirds of the tusk is solid ivory.

- An elephant's teeth determine how long it will live. Only six sets of molars can grow during an elephant's lifetime. Once the last set is worn down, the elephant can no longer chew properly, and will slowly starve to death. The elephant lives an average of 55 to 60 years.

- Elephants have very small eyes protected by long lashes on the upper lid. Their vision is poor, so they rely on their sense of smell.

- An adult elephant drinks up to 150 quarts (165 l) of water a day, and eats 2000 mouthfuls of soft wood, bark, greenery and fruit to satisfy its hunger. They need to eat 200-500 pounds (90-227 kg) of vegetation daily, depending on their size.

- Grown bull elephants wrestle each other for rank in the herd. The winner is boss.

- An elephant spreads its ears widely as a sign of danger. Most of its enemies will run away at the giant's first attacking steps.

SUMMARY

To exist, language has to have three qualities: (1) it must express a meaning or some content, (2) it must have some form, and (3) it is used purposefully. As we teach thematically, all of what we do requires us to use language, and the children's responses require them to try to use language. As children demonstrate a need for language skills, these are taught and practiced.

To teach thematically means accepting most of the following set of beliefs:

1. Language exists to express meanings.

2. Language skills evolve from trying to make sense of the speech and print of the world into which we are born.

3. Literacy skills improve through practice. The practice must be purposeful. Children read to learn with the results that they learn to read. Children write to record what they are learning to communicate with others with the result that they learn to write.

4. There is no absolute sequence in which skills are learned or need to be taught.

5. Language learning is a social, non-competitive process.

6. The minimum text that may be used to teach reading is the whole book, chapter, poem, or story.

7. There is no disintegration of language into components for daily teaching.

8. Reading is done through apprehension. The brain directs the eye to make sense of a mass of text.

9. All children go through the same stages in learning to read and write, at different times and at different learning rates, of course.

10. All children are capable of literacy if they do not become confused or frustrated in learning *how print works.* Almost all children require direct, sensitive teaching if they are to learn *how print works.*

Thematic teaching is not easy, but no good teaching is. When themes are used, the children concentrate upon learning content, and as the children work with language, the teacher teaches the necessary skills and sets the children to practicing those skills as they record what they are learning. Thematic teaching is *responsive teaching* — the teacher listens to children's responses, and observes their behavior as they respond and practice. Finally, thematic teaching has the potential for being so rewarding that the work required will seem justified.

Bibliography of Books for Children

Alborough, Jez. *Esther's Trunk: An Elephantasy*. London: Walker Books, 1988.

Barner, Bob. *Elephant Facts*. New York: Dutton, 1979.

Barrett, Norman S. *Elephants*. New York: Franklin Watts, 1988. (A Picture Book)

Barton, Byron. *Elephant*. New York: Seabury Press, 1971.

Bayley, Nicola. *Elephant Cat*. New York: Knopf, Random House, 1984.

Bos, Burny. *Ollie the Elephant*. New York: North-South Books, 1989.

Bright, Michael. *Elephants*. New York: Gloucester Press, 1990.

Brown, Margaret Wise. *The Important Book*. New York: Harper & Row, 1949.

_____. "I Like Bugs." In *The Fish With the Deep Sea Smile: Stories and Poems for Reading to Young Children*. Hamden, CT: Linnet Books, 1988.

Bruna, Dick. *The Dog*. New York: Thomas Y. Crowell, 1975.

———. *My Shirt Is White*. London: Methuen, 1973.

Burmingham, John. *Would You Rather?* New York: Thomas Y. Crowell, 1978.

Burns, Florence M. *Jumbo, the Biggest Elephant in the World*. Richmond Hill, ON: Scholastic-TAB, 1978.

Burton, Marilee. *Tail Toes Eyes Ears Nose*. New York: Harper and Row, 1988.

Caple, Kathy. *The Biggest Nose*. Boston: Houghton Mifflin, 1985.

Carle, Eric. *The Very Hungry Caterpillar*. New York: Philomel, 1969.

Carrick, Carol. *The Elephant in the Dark*. New York: Clarion Books, 1988.

Cork, Barbara Taylor. *Elephants*. Toronto: Kids Can Press, 1989.

Cowcher, Helen. *Antarctica*. Farrar, New York: Straus and Giroux, 1990.

Cuming, Peter. *Mogul and Me*. Charlottetown, PEI: Ragweed, 1989.

Daly, Maureen. *Rosie, The Dancing Elephant*. New York: Dodd, Mead, 1967.

De Brunhoff, Laurent. *Babar's Picnic*. New York: Random House, 1991.

De Brunhoff, Jean. *The Travels of Babar*. New York: Dragonfly Books, Alfred A. Knopf, 1934.

Delacre, Lulu. *Nathan and Nicholas Alexander*. New York: Scholastic, 1986.

———. *Time for School, Nathan!* New York: Scholastic, 1989.

———. *Nathan's Balloon Adventure*. New York: Scholastic, 1991.

Delton, Judy. *The Elephant in Duck's Garden*. Niles, IL: A. Whitman, 1985.

De Watterville, Vivienne. *Speak to the Earth*. New York: W.W. Norton, 1987.

Dingwall, Laima, and Annabel Slaight, eds. "The Brave Emperor." In *OWL Magazine*, Toronto, 1980.

Dowell, Ruth I. *Move Over Mother Goose*. Mt. Ranier, MD: Gryphon House, 1987.

Eberle, Irmengarde. *Elephants Live Here*. New York, 1970.

Ele, J. *Elephants*. New York: Gloucester Press. 1979.

Fox, Mem. *Hattie and the Fox*. New York: Bradbury Press, 1987.

———. *Shoes from Grampa*. New York: Orchard Press, 1990.

Freedman, Russell. *Sharks*. New York: Holiday House, 1985.

Freeman, Dan. *Elephants, the Vanishing Giants*. New York: Putnam, 1982.

Gibbons, Gail. *The Puffins Are Back*. New York: HarperCollins, 1991.

Ginsburg, Mirra. *The Chick and the Duckling*. New York: Macmillan, 1972.

———. *Where Does the Sun Go At Night?* New York: Greenwillow, 1981.

Goodall, Jane, ed. Animal World series. New York: Atheneum, 1990.

Grambling, Lois. *Elephant and Mouse Celebrate Halloween*. New York: Barron's, 1991.

Hall, Derek. *Elephant Bathes*. London: Walker Books, 1985.

Harper, Wilhelmina. *Gunniwolf*. New York: E.P. Dutton, 1964.

Hawkins, Colin, and Jacqui Hawkins. *The Elephant*. New York: Viking Kestrel, 1985.

Heller, Ruth. *Animals Born Alive and Well*. New York: Grosset and Dunlap, 1981.

———. *Chickens Aren't the Only Ones*. New York: Grosset and Dunlap, 1982.

Hoban, Russell. *The Twenty-Elephant Restaurant*. New York: Atheneum, 1978.

Hoffman, Mary. *Elephant*. Milwaukee: Raintree Children's Books, 1984.

Holbrook, John. *A Closer Look at Elephants*. New York: Franklin Watts, 1977.

Hoppe, Matthias. *Mouse and Elephant*. Boston: Little, Brown and Co., 1990.

Hutchins, Pat. *Rosie's Walk*. New York: Macmillan, 1968.

———. *Good Night, Owl*. New York: Macmillan, 1972.

Jacobs, Leland. *Good Night, Mr. Beetle*. New York: Holt, Rinehart & Winston.

Joyce, Susan. *Peel — The Extraordinary Elephant*. Portland, OR: Peel Productions, 1988.

Jurmain, Suzanne. *From Trunk to Tail: Elephants Legendary and Real*. New York: Harcourt Brace Jovanovich, 1978.

Kamal, Aleph. *The Bird Who Was an Elephant*. New York: J.P. Lippincott, 1989.

Kaza, Keiko. *When the Elephant Walks*. New York: Putman, 1990.

Kelsey, Reinhard. *Elephants*. New York: Abradale Press, 1981.

Kent, Jack. *Fat Cat*. Toronto: Scholastic, 1971.

King, Deborah. *Puffin*. Lothrop, Lee and Shepard: New York, 1984.

Kipling, Rudyard. *The Elephant's Child*. New York: Doubleday, 1912.

Kraus, Robert. *Whose Mouse Are You?* New York: Macmillan, 1970.

———. *Boris Bad Enough*. New York: Simon and Schuster, 1976.

Krauss, Ruth. *The Happy Egg*. Toronto: Scholastic, 1967.

Kuskin, Karla. *Dogs and Dragons, Trees and Dreams*. New York: Harper and Row, 1980.

Lane, Margaret. *The Frog, The Squirrel, The Beaver, The Fish, The Fox*, and *The Spider*. New York: Dial Press, 1982.

Lavine, Sigmund A. *Wonders of Elephants*. New York: Dodd, Mead, 1979.

Lee, Dennis. *Alligator Pie*. Toronto: Macmillan, 1974. (Music by Raffi in "Singable Songbook," New York: Crown Publishers, 1987.)

Lenski, Lois. *Lois Lenski's Big Book of Mr. Small.* New York: H.Z. Walck, 1979.

_____. *More Mr. Small.* New York: H.Z. Walck, 1979.

_____. *Lois Lenski's Big Big Book of Mr. Small.* New York: Derrydale Books, 1985.

Leydenfrost, Robert. *Ten Little Elephants.* Garden City, NY: Doubleday, 1925. Imprint 1975.

Lobel, Arnold. *Uncle Elephant.* New York: Scholastic, 1981.

Marshall, Henry Neil. *Elephant Kingdom.* London: Hale, 1959.

Martin, Bill Jr. *Brown Bear, Brown Bear, What Do You See?* New York: Holt, Rinehart and Winston, 1967.

Mayer, Mercer. *Ah-Choo.* New York: Dial Books, 1976.

McClung, Robert. *Gorilla.* New York: Wm. Morrow, 1984.

———. *Hunted Mammals of the Sea.* New York: Wm. Morrow, 1978.

———. *Rajpur: Last of the Bengal Tigers.* New York: Wm. Morrow, 1982.

———. *America's First Elephant.* New York: Morrow Junior Books, 1991.

McCracken, Robert A. and Marlene J. McCracken. *The Fat Pig, The Old Woman and the Pig, Little Fish, The Grand Old Duke of York,* and *A Hen Can.* Surrey, BC: McCracken Educational Services; Winnipeg: Peguis Publishers, 1986-1989.

———. *The Farmer and the Skunk, How Do You Say Hello to a Ghost?, Where Do You Live?, What Do You Have?, Some Dogs Don't* et al. Tiger Cub Books. Winnipeg: Peguis Publishers, 1991.

———. *Hiding From The Cold, Little Yellow Duck, The Big Red Barn, The Big Red Apple, I Am a Pirate, Children's Alphabet, Animal Rap, The Fly in the Barnyard,* and *Spider on the Floor.* Surrey, BC: McCracken Educational Services, 1989-91.

McKee, David Elmer. *The Story of a Patchwork Elephant*. New York: Lothrop, 1991.

McPhail, David. *Where Can an Elephant Hide?* New York: Doubleday, 1979.

Michel, Anna. *Little Wild Elephant*. New York: Pantheon, 1979.

Milne, A. A. "At the Zoo." In *When We Were Very Young*. New York: Dutton, 1924.

Moon, Cliff. *Elephants in the Wild*. Hove, East Sussex, England: Wayland, 1984.

Muldoon, Guy. *The Trumpeting Herd*. London: Hart-Davis, 1957.

Murray, Neil. *The Love of Elephants*. London: Octopus Books, 1976.

Neitzel, Shirley. *The Jacket I Wore in the Snow*. New York: Greenwillow Books, 1989.

nicol, bp. *Once: A Lullabye*. New York: Greenwillow Books, 1983.

Nikola-Lisa, W. *Night is Coming*. New York: Dutton Children's Books, 1991.

Numeroff, Laura Joffe. *If You Give a Moose a Muffin*. New York: HarperCollins, 1991.

Overbeck, Cynthia. *Elephants*. Minneapolis: Lerner Publications, Co., 1981.

Pallotta, Jerry. *The Icky Bug Alphabet Book, The Bird Alphabet Book, The Ocean Alphabet Book, The Flower Alphabet Book, The Yucky Reptile Alphabet Book*, and *The Frog Alphabet Book* Watertown, MA: Charlesbridge, 1989.

Pearce, Philipps. *Emily's Own Elephant*. London: J. MacRae Books, 1987.

Peet, Bill. *Ella*. New York: Houghton Mifflin, 1964.

———. *Encore for Elephant*. Boston: Houghton Mifflin, 1981.

Pepper, Dennis. *The Elephant Book*. Oxford, Toronto: Oxford University Press, 1983.

Posell, Elsa Z. *Elephants*. Chicago: Children's Press, 1982.

Prelutsky, Jack. *Ride a Purple Pelican*. New York: Greenwillow Books, 1986.

――――. *Beneath the Blue Umbrella*. New York: Greenwillow Books, 1990.

Project Puffin. Learning Corp. of America, Audubon Society film, (16 mm), 30 min.

Rao, Udiavar, G. *Elephant Baby*. Chicago: Encyclopedia Britannica Press in association with Meredith Press, Des Moines, 1962.

Ravielle, Anthony. *Elephants, the Last of the Land Giants*. New York: Parent's Magazine Press, 1965.

Rettich, Margret. *Suleiman the Elephant*. New York: Lothrop, Lee & Shepard Books, 1984.

Richardson, Judith Benet. *The Way Home*. New York: Macmillan, 1991.

Riddell, Chris. *The Trouble With Elephants*. New York: Lippincott, 1988.

Rogers, Edmund. *Elephants*. New York: Raintree Children's Books, 1977.

Roth, Susan L. *We'll Ride Elephants Through Brooklyn*. New York: Farrar, Straus and Giroux, 1989.

Ryder, Joanne. *The Spider's Dance*. New York: Harper & Row, 1981.

――――. *The Snail's Spell*. New York: Viking, 1992.

Schlein, Miriam. *Elephants*. (in Jane Goodall's *Animal World*) New York: Atheneum, 1990.

Sendak, Maurice. Nutshell Library series. New York: Harper & Row, 1962.

Shannon, George. *Lizard's Song*. New York: Greenwillow Books, 1981.

———. *Dance Away.* New York: Greenwillow Books, 1982.

Sheppard, Jill. *The Right Number of Elephants.* New York: Harper and Row, 1990.

Simon, Mina Lewiton. *Is Anyone There?* New York: Atheneum, 1967; Toronto: McClelland and Stewart, 1967.

Slobodkina, Esphyr. *The Three Billy Goats Gruff.* New York: Wm. R. Scott, 1940, 1947.

Smath, Jerry. *But No Elephants.* New York: Harper and Row, 1990.

Stidworthy, John, and Hewitt Rosalind. *A Year in the Life.* New York: Silver Burdett, 1987.

Stock, Catherine. *Alexander's Midnight Snack: A Little Elephant's ABC.* New York: Clarion Books, 1988.

Stong, Philip Duffield. *A Beast Called an Elephant.* New York: Dodd, Mead, 1955.

Sutton, Eve. *My Cat Likes to Hide in Boxes.* Barnstaple, Devon: Spindlewood, 1984.

Taylor, J. David. *The Elephant and the Scrubforest.* Toronto: Crabtree Publishing Co., 1990.

The Old Woman who Swallowed a Fly. Traditional. Surrey, BC: McCracken Educational Services, 1984.

Titherington, Jeanne. *Pumpkin Pumpkin.* Greenwillow: New York, 1986.

Tresselt, Alvin. *Sun Up.* New York: Lothrop, Lee & Shepard, 1991.

Tsuchiya, Yukio. *Faithful Elephants: A True Story of Animals, People and War.* Boston: Houghton Mifflin, 1988.

Van Wormer, Joe. *Elephants.* New York: Dutton, 1976.

Vevers, Gwynne. *Elephants and Mammoths*, London: Bodley Head 1968.

Vipont, Elfrida. *The Elephant and the Bad Baby.* New York: Coward-McCann, 1969.

Waddell, Martin. *The Day It Rained Elephants.* London: Methuen Children's Books, 1986.

Waldeck, Theodore J. *Jamba the Elephant.* New York: Viking Press: 1942.

Wax, Wendy. *Ten Things I Know About Elephants.* Chicago: Contemporary Books, 1990.

West, Colin. *One Little Elephant.* New York: Barron's, 1988.

Wexo, John B. Zoo Books, *Elephants.* San Diego: Wildlife Education Ltd., 1980.

Wildsmith, Brian. *The Trunk.* Toronto: Oxford, 1982.

————. *Cat on the Mat.* Toronto: Oxford, 1982.

Wood, Don and Audrey. *The Napping House.* New York: Harcourt Brace Jovanovich, 1984.

Yoshida, Toshi. *Elephant Crossing.* New York: Philomel Books, 1984.

Zemach, Harve. *The Judge: An Untrue Tale.* New York: Farrar, Straus and Giroux, 1969.

Bibliography of Professional References

Adams, M.J. *Beginning to Read: Thinking and Learning About Print*. Cambridge, MA: The MIT Press, 1990.

Ashton-Warner, Sylvia. *Spinster*. New York: Simon & Schuster, 1959.

———. *Teacher*. New York: Simon & Schuster, 1963.

Bettelheim, Bruno. *The Uses of Enchantment*. New York: Alfred Knopf, 1976: 18-19.

Brooke, Mona. *Drawing with Children*. Los Angeles: Jeremy P. Tarcher, 1986.

Butler, Dorothy. *Cushla and Her Books*. Boston: The Horn Book, 1980.

Carson, Rachel. *Sense of Wonder*. New York: Harper and Row, 1956: 5, 8, 45.

Clay, Marie. *Reading: The Patterning of Complex Behaviour*. Auckland, N.Z.: Heinemann, 1972.

———. *The Early Detection of Reading Difficulties*. Auckland, N.Z.: Heinemann, 1979.

Cramer, Ronald L. Unpublished manuscript. Rochester Hills, MI: Oakland University, n.d.

Durkin, Dolores. *Children Who Read Early*. New York: Teachers College Press, 1966.

Flesch, Rudolph. *Why Johnny Can't Read*. New York: Harper, 1955.

Holdaway, Don. *The Foundation of Literacy*. Toronto: Ashton Scholastic, 1979.

Jennings, Frank. *This Is Reading*. Bureau of Publications, Teachers College, Columbia University: New York, 1965.

McCracken, Marlene J., and Robert A. McCracken. *Spelling Through Phonics*. Winnipeg: Peguis Publishers, 1982.

McCracken, Marlene J. *Spelling* (video). Surrey, BC: McCracken Educational Services, 1990.

Smith, Frank. *Writing and the Writer.* New York: Holt, Rinehart and Winston, 1982.

Wells, Gordon. *The Meaning Makers, Children Learning Language and Using Language to Learn.* Portsmouth, NH: Heinemann, 1986.